May the —

Fingerprints of GOD

be with you always!

O. A. Fish

Prov. 3:5-6

O. A. FISH
WITH LINDA TOMBLIN

BROADMAN P[RESS]
NASHVILLE, TENN[ESSEE]

D0720805

© Copyright 1990 ● Broadman Press
All Rights Reserved
4250-86

ISBN: 0-8054-5086-6
Dewey Decimal Classification: 248.842
Subject Headings: RELIGIOUS LIFE // WITNESSING // FISH, O. A.
Library of Congress Catalog Number: 89-48572

Printed in the United States of America

The article included in chapter 31 of this book, "Charbel Yones and the Voice of Hope" by O. A. Fish, originally appeared in *Power for Living* magazine July 7, 1985 (first rights).

Library of Congress Cataloging-in-Publication Data

Fish, O. A., 1934-
    Fingerprints of God / O.A. Fish with Linda Tomblin.
    p. cm.
    ISBN 0-8054-5086-6
    1. Fish, O. A., 1934- . 2. Baptists--United States--Biography.
3. Air pilots--United States--Biography, 4. Witness bearing
(Christianity) I. Tomblin, Linda, 1941- . II. Title.
    BX6495.F47A3 1990
286'.1'092--dc
[B]

89-48572
CIP

To the delight of my wife, Charlotte, and our daughters, Cheryl, Lisa, and Kimberly, I dedicate this book to the loving memory of our daughter Barbara Jean. Amidst our pain at the loss of Barbara, each of us in unique ways has experienced the fingerprints of God.

What They're Saying About
Fingerprints of God

PAT BOONE, Hollywood, California . . . "I fly almost constantly, it seems; and though I commit my life into God's hands every
flight, it thrills me when I discover that the captain of the airliner
is a Spirit-filled, dedicated Christian. Reading O. A. Fish's warm
and wonderful story fills me with a peculiar and special joy."

JAMIE BUCKINGHAM, *Ministries Today* magazine . . . "Captain
Fish sees world events from the perspective of a pilot looking
down from high places. These exciting stories are really ancient
prophecies fulfilled today."

GEORGE OTIS, High Adventure Ministries, Voice of Hope International Radio Network . . . "The manuscript set my heart
pounding. The pen of the Captain flashes with fingerprints of an
exciting Maker flying the skyways and walking the earth. Nobody
ever told it better."

BEN KINCHLOW, Ben Kinchlow Ministries, former co-host of
"The 700 Club" . . . "Tremendous! At the scene of the crime
there is no evidence until an examination clearly reveals the fingerprints of the culprit. In the case of our lives we may not see
the presence of God at first glance, until the evidence clearly
reveals the fingerprints of God. In the case of Captain Fish,
there is no question that the *Fingerprints* of God are obvious even
to the casual observer. God has been there."

Contents

Preface

For since the creation of the world God's invisible qualities—his eternal power and divine nature—have been clearly seen, being understood from what has been made, so that men are without excuse [for knowing Him] (Rom. 1:20).

From the lofty captain's seat of a commercial airliner,
where I am privileged to fly, I feel so small
and insignificant—dwarfed by the view out my cockpit window.

It is a clear night as I gaze out into the vastness
of our universe, and there stirs within me a question:
From what source come the wonders I behold?

I remember the thousands of sunrises and sunsets
which my eyes have feasted on. Each a unique panorama
of artistic beauty, painted in celebration
to separate the darkness from the day.
Who is the masterful artist who never
bores us with the same painting twice?

Even when back down to earth, there is always
a lump in my throat when I see some gentleman
ease an elderly lady's burden by offering to carry her bags.
What possesses him to perform such a kindly deed?

Then there is the intrigue when
an unhappy baby's mother squeezes it to her loving breast,
and the baby's cry becomes a cuddly coo.
What is the magic of her touch?

Surely such splendor, such beauty, such caring, such love
has a common source, doesn't it?
From deep within my spirit, the answer comes:
These are but "the fingerprints of God."

—O. A. Fish

Part 1:
The Flowering of Faith

But as many as received him, to them gave he power to become the sons of God (John 1:12, KJV).

For as many as are led by the Spirit of God, they are the sons of God (Rom. 8:14, KJV).

Although John 1:12 gives us the power to do so, some Christians mature into the position of sonship as described in Romans 8:14 faster than others. I guess I would have to be classified as one of those slow growers, and Part 1 of *Fingerprints of God* tells of my maturing process from Christian infancy to grown-up sonship.

1

When the Music Stops

For I am convinced that neither death nor life, neither angels nor demons, neither the present nor the future, nor any powers, neither height nor depth, nor anything else in all creation, will be able to separate us from the love of God that is in Christ Jesus our Lord (Rom. 8:38-39).

I strained to see the center line as I drove my pickup toward the airport. It was New Year's Eve, and the cold winter rain was covering the windshield almost as fast as the wipers pushed it away. "Sure is a bad night for the kids to be driving home." I mumbled. It wasn't the first time I'd talked to myself on the trip between my home in Bostic, North Carolina, and the Greenville-Spartanburg Airport in South Carolina. I was a captain with Eastern Airlines, and I made the trip more often than I liked to think about. However, it was usually a good time to catch up on my thoughts or plan the coming week. But that night, I had more on my mind than next week's schedule or even the fact that I was running late.

Our two teenage daughters, Barbara and Cheryl, and some Christian friends had spent the last several days at a Christmas conference sponsored by Campus Crusade for Christ in Georgia; I knew at that moment they were probably somewhere on that same highway on their way home. Barbara was a good driver, but I couldn't help worrying with the downpour and holiday celebrants combined. I kept hoping I would pass them at some point along the road. At least, then I would know they were almost home.

I tried to tell myself I had to stop looking for them and concentrate on getting to the airport, but I couldn't get out of my

mind what Barbara said the night before when she called. I
could tell she had been crying. "Mom, . . . Dad," she said, "I just
wanted to tell you that I love you . . . and . . ." she hesitated for a
second. "I don't know why, but I don't feel like I'm ever going to
get home." Her mother and I tried to comfort her and assure
her that we'd see her the next day, but then I'd suddenly got
called out for this unexpected flight. And alone in my truck that
evening, her words kept beating in my ears, keeping some crazy
kind of rhythm with the rain pounding against the windshield.

The weather had caused my drive to take longer than usual,
and when I reached the airport, I didn't have time to think about
the kids or anything else except catching my flight to Atlanta—
my home base. Then, when I finally reached Atlanta, I was assigned to connect on another flight to Tampa where an Eastern
DC 9 was awaiting a fresh crew. Since the weather had delayed
our arrival into Atlanta, once I got there I had to rush straight to
the departure gate for the Tampa-bound plane.

The flight had just closed out with every passenger seat filled,
so I breathed a sigh of relief as I buckled myself into the jump
seat, which is a spare observer's seat in the cockpit. I hadn't had
a chance to even introduce myself to the crew when the passen-
ger-loading jetway started moving back from the plane. But
then, suddenly, it stopped and started moving slowly back to
the plane's entrance door.

The gate agent stuck his head into the plane and glanced
around. His eyes stopped on me. "Are you Captain Fish?" he
asked.

"Yes, I am," I answered.

"Would you bring your bags please, Captain, and come with
me? Crew scheduling needs to talk to you."

He turned and held the door, waiting for me. I looked at the
astonished senior flight attendant and shrugged, "Doesn't that
beat all? They must have gotten someone else to cover the flight
since I was running late."

I hurriedly climbed the stairs to the second floor above the
terminal concourse where crew scheduling offices were located.
I was a bit irritated that I had come all the way from North Carolina on a rainy New Year's Eve just to be replaced. I couldn't

think of any other reason they would have called me back. But when I walked into the office, Bobby, the scheduling supervisor, handed me a slip of paper with a telephone number on it. "We've been asked to have you call your brother," he told me. But when I reached for the phone on his desk, he stopped me. "Better use the one in there," he said, motioning toward an office in the rear.

"Hello." My brother's deep voice answered on the first ring.

"Eugene, what's wrong?" I asked. "Has something happened?"

"I . . . I'm afraid so," he stammered. "There's been an accident . . . when the kids were coming home." I knew he was having trouble explaining, but I was having even more difficulty standing there waiting for him to finish.

"Eugene, are the girls all right?" I interrupted.

"Well, I'm afraid that Barbara . . ." his voice faded away. Then it came back, "O. A., I'm sorry, but Barbara is gone. She was killed."

I opened my mouth to protest, but nothing came out. I could feel myself sinking into a chair beside the desk. Somewhere in the distance, Eugene's voice was calling me. "O. A., O. A., can you hear me?"

I struggled but finally forced myself to respond. "Yes, Eugene I hear you."

"Cheryl is in the hospital," he said. "They don't know how serious her injuries are yet. She only arrived a short while ago. Charlotte called me and asked that I locate you."

He gave me the hospital's number, and the next few minutes were spent sharing with my wife in a private sorrow that only a mother and father can experience in such a time. After assuring her that I would be home as soon as possible, I returned to the outer office. As I picked up my suitcase and started toward the door, I could see several of the schedulers and pilots move toward me and then stop, as though they'd just realized they wouldn't know what to do if they reached me. Turning back, I gave them a slight wave and stepped out into the pilot's mail room. There I stopped and leaned against a row of mail boxes; I was alone, so alone. My mind whirled as I tried to let the news sink in. Some tough things had come my way before, but never anything like that ache inside. It was threatening to swallow me whole.

"God," I sighed, "You're going to have to help me. I just don't understand. I don't want to question you, but Lord, I'm hurting so bad." A calmness and acceptance began to slowly fold around me. It was much like the feeling I remembered as a child when I would get hurt, and Dad would pick me up, dust me off, and give me a hug. There was a real sense that my Heavenly Father was now doing the same. The ache didn't go away; it was still there, but knowing that He loved me and cared that I was hurting helped. A familiar Scripture then began to scroll through my mind: "We know that all things work together for good to them that love God" (Rom. 8:28, KJV). The grip of God's loving arms seemed to tighten around me as I yielded to Him. "I still don't understand, Lord," I cried. "But somehow I know that this promise is for me." And so it was in that deepest wound I'd ever experienced, I could feel my Heavenly Father's loving embrace.

In the rapture of the moment, I could almost see Barbara running across heaven and into the outstretched arms of Jesus. A warm joy and a feeling like silken lace began to slip down over my head and engulf my body, bringing with it a peace like I'd never experienced before. "I give her to You, Lord," I whispered. "I give her to You." And I meant it. I believe that had I been given the choice at that moment, I would not have asked for her back.

A hand on my arm startled me, and I looked up to see another Eastern captain. I had seen him many times before, but I didn't know his name. "Come on, O. A.," he said. "There's a plane leaving for Greenville, and we're holding it for you." He hurried me downstairs and into a waiting ramp service pickup truck. And as we drove across the parking apron, I saw a DC 9 with its engines running and its steps down waiting for me to arrive. I still couldn't talk to anyone, but I mumbled something like thanks to him, jumped out of the pickup, and ran up the aircraft's front loading stairs. The senior flight attendant seated me next to her on the forward flight attendant jump seat.

The plane was filled with passengers celebrating New Year's Eve. The flight had been delayed for about an hour because of the weather, and they were in high spirits by the time I climbed on board. But I just kind of slid down into the jump seat, laid my head back, and closed my eyes. I didn't want to see anything or anybody. I just wanted the plane to hurry up, taxi out, and feel that familiar surge of power which meant we were on our way to Greenville before I opened my eyes again.

We were delayed a bit longer, waiting for ground control clearance to taxi to the runway. I was sitting there trying not to think when I heard a voice in front of me. Wearily I opened my eyes and glanced up to find a passenger standing there staring down at me. "Hey, everybody," he yelled to his friends. "Look at the sad little captain." He bent over, his eyes just inches from mine. "What's wrong, sad little captain? Don't you know it's New Year's Eve? You're not supposed to be sad!" He reached down for my arm, trying to entice me to join in their festivities.

"You'd be sad too," I replied as I slowly pried his hand from my arm, "if you'd just gotten news that your teenage daughter had been killed in an automobile accident." The silence spread like an icy wave over the plane. The obnoxious passenger fell to his knees in the galley floor beside me.

"Oh!" he gasped, "I'm sorry! I'm so sorry!" For the first time in his life, probably, he had nothing else to say. Tears filled his eyes as I reached out my hand to help him up. I knew that God was showing me Barbara's death would be a means of reaching out to others and extending His love. And someday, I knew, I'd be able to look back and see His touch in that devastating loss, just the way I'd seen Him in other areas of my life.

Moments later, a pastor who was sitting in the first-class section passed a note to me telling me that he was praying for me and my family, which showed me that His love would also be extended to me through others.

My brother Doug met me at the Greenville-Spartanburg Airport and drove me home. As I moved through the crowd who had gathered at our house, I was greatly relieved to see Cheryl lying on the couch in our den with her right arm in a sling. I rushed over and knelt beside her. "You don't have to worry about me, Dad," she said. "All I have is a cracked collarbone, and the rest of the kids are all right too." She lay back and smiled at me weakly, "And you know, Dad, you don't have to worry about Barbara either—because she's in heaven."

I had been praying all the way home that God's grace would be on my family, and He had answered that prayer even before I'd arrived. Our neighbors and friends had kind of taken charge. Food was pouring in, and our every need was being met before we could even ask. We were receiving calls from as far away as the Philippines as our network of friends around the world began passing the word.

It was after two o'clock in the morning before Charlotte and I finally got to bed, even then it took a while for my mind to relax. But when I finally dozed off, some time during the short night I started dreaming of a heavenly choir. They were singing beautiful, old familiar hymns—comforting songs—the kind we had sung when I was young and the kind sung at my father's funeral. The words and music were bringing me such encouragement and comfort that even in my dream I kept hoping they wouldn't stop; somehow I knew if I could only keep the words of those hymns in mind, I could make it. But I shouldn't have worried, because when I dragged myself out of bed to face the unpleasant tasks of the day, I suddenly realized the music was still there—in soft stereo inside my head. The morning sun didn't fade it. The conversations of friends didn't drown it out. It just kept going, through the receiving of friends at the funeral home, during the funeral, and for several days afterward. All my thoughts and actions were tinted by the music floating through my head. The words and melodies dulled the sharp edge of death for me in a way nothing else could have done. God knew that, but He also knew that the music was only a reprieve—the time would come when He would have to take it away.

It was about four days after Barbara's funeral when it happened. I was sitting alone, meditating with my Bible lying open on my lap. It was opened to my favorite section—the eighth chapter of Romans. I was remembering how God had helped me to recall the twenty-eighth verse the day Barbara died. As I whispered the words to myself, "We know that in all things God works for the good," I could feel the music begin to slide away. "Please, God, not yet," I begged silently. "I'm not ready to stand alone; I still need . . ."

But it was as though God stopped me in mid-sentence. I sensed Him speaking to my spirit, *"You won't need the music any longer. All you'll ever need is in your Bible."* I looked down and began to read . . . hesitantly . . . still uncertain. But the question in verse 35 caught my attention. "Who shall separate us from the love of Christ?" I wanted to hurry and find the answer, but instead I found myself reading slowly, savoring each word. "Shall trouble or hardship or persecution or famine or nakedness or danger or sword? . . . No, in all these things we are more than conquerors through him who loved us. For I am convinced that neither death nor life," I stopped, took a deep breath, and reread the last few words. But this time, I read them out loud, gaining courage and strength from each syllable. "Neither death nor life, neither angels nor demons, neither the present nor the future, nor any powers, neither height nor depth, nor anything else in all creation, will be able to separate us from the love of God that is in Christ Jesus our Lord." My spirit soaked up the words like a dry sponge, and by the time I'd finished reading them, I was ready to say, "You're right, Lord. I don't need the music anymore." And the melody stopped.

Furthermore, I have found since that day that His promise has remained true. I am constantly aware of His ever-present love, and I know that nothing can separate me from it. This "knowing" came to me as a gift, but I am convinced it is available to everyone who will reach out for it. He is all around us—right beside us—closer even than our own bodies. If we will let Him, He will walk with us daily, give us music when we need it, and when the time comes—as it often does—that He must take the melody away, then He will give us something stronger to which we may cling.

2

Wounded Faith

He [Jesus] called a little child and had him stand among them. And he said: "I tell you the truth, unless you change and become like little children, you will never enter the kingdom of heaven. Therefore, whoever humbles himself like this child is the greatest in the kingdom of heaven" (Matt. 18:2-4).

It had been a long time coming, but I knew that day as I sat alone with God and was able to let Him take the music away that I had finally returned full cycle to the simple faith I had known as a child.

I was next to the oldest of ten children born to Otho Alden, Sr., and Pauline Fish. The average age between my brothers and sisters was two years. We were a large and loving family, and we were taught to believe in God. From as far back as I could remember, He was a personal friend to me—a truth I never thought to question. When we lived on Reid Street in the little town of Forest City, North Carolina, I would set up an orange crate for a pulpit and preach to the alcoholics who sometimes staggered down our street. Then when I was nine, my Aunt Maude took me to an old-fashioned tent revival meeting. It was there that I invited Jesus to come into my heart. I knelt down in the wood shavings by a homemade altar and followed the preacher as he led me in the sinner's prayer.

"God forgive me of my sins," I prayed. "And Lord Jesus come into my heart, save me, cause me to be the person You want me to be." It was just a simple prayer, but there was no room for doubt in my childlike faith.

However, that faith in a personal intervening God began to

dwindle during my early teens. It was during an especially difficult time when it seemed God was not listening to my prayers.
Death was threatening to destroy our family—one member at a
time—while I stood by helplessly and watched. Mama's older
brother, Jesse, was the first one to die during a short period of
three years. Then her father, my beloved Grandpa Padgett,
slipped away; her older brother, Will, was found to be terminally
ill—all of them with cancer. But the hardest of all to face was
when my father became ill. He had been suffering for several
years with high blood pressure, and he had already suffered a
couple of strokes which had left him slightly paralyzed.

One night when I had just gotten home from visiting my Uncle Will and was trying to sneak into the house without awakening the family, the final faith-killing blow struck. We were living
·in the country at that time, and Uncle Will lived in a small farm
house just a few miles from us. Knowing how sick Uncle Will
was, I liked to go see him as often as I could. The two-story farm
house we lived in was about fifty years old, so I opened the
screen door carefully, hoping the inevitable squeak wouldn't
wake my parents or new baby brother. Mama always slept with
each new baby until another one arrived. Mama, Dad, my three
sisters, and the baby slept in the living room while my brothers
and I slept in the room next to them. To keep from disturbing
the rest of the family, I tiptoed in without turning on the lights.
But just as I passed the living room door, Daddy jumped out
from behind it and hollered, "Boo!" Apparently he had been
sleeping in our room because the baby had been keeping him
awake, and he had heard me coming in. I almost jumped out of
my skin, and we both fell back against the wall laughing our
heads off. It was a great moment. I had been worried about him
for such a long time, yet there he was—the same old fun-loving
Dad he had always been. Seeing him joking and laughing lifted
the depressed feeling I'd brought home with me from Uncle
Will's.

In fact, I felt better than I had in months as I pulled off my
blue jeans and crawled into bed. I had just gotten settled down
under the covers, when I heard my mother scream. I grabbed my
pants and struggled into them as I ran into their room. The girls

were sitting up in bed, rubbing their eyes and trying to figure out what was happening. Mama was sitting there on her knees on the bed, her fists pressed to her mouth as if to stifle the screams that still hung in the air. Daddy lay next to her gasping for breath. She turned to me yelling, "Junior, get a doctor!" We had no telephone, and the nearest neighbors who did have one were the Carpenters that lived about a quarter of a mile away. I ran out the door as fast as I could, but it seemed as if I were crawling down the dirt road. I couldn't seem to make my legs go quickly enough. When I reached the Carpenter's house and finally woke them up, I was so out of breath and anxious that I could hardly tell her what was wrong.

Mrs. Carpenter called the doctor and made me sit down and rest for a few minutes. She tried her best to calm me down before letting me leave. When she did let me go, I ran as fast as I could. By the time I got to the house, the doctor was already there sitting astride my dad, trying to help him breathe. I knew it was bad, and I couldn't stand to watch, so I ran out the door and climbed into our old '36 Chevrolet. I sat there alone, crying and praying harder than I'd ever prayed before. I knew Daddy was dying just like Grandpa and Uncle Jesse had done. "Please God," I pleaded. "Please help him." Finally, exhausted, I fell asleep; sometime later, I was awakened by my younger sister Dorcus, who was pecking on the car window. "Junior, Junior," she sobbed, "Daddy's dead."

I couldn't make myself go back into the house that night. Instead, I went to my Aunt Lorene's who lived close by. And even the next day, I wouldn't go home. I couldn't stand the thought of seeing my dad, lying there in a casket. I wanted to remember him alive, laughing, and joking—the way he'd been just minutes before that fatal stroke.

That night my childlike faith went out the window. I felt God had let me down. When Uncle Will died a few months later, I wasn't even surprised. It wasn't that I had quit believing in God. I just no longer believed He would intervene in our personal lives.

It took years before I began to look for—and eventually recognize—God's fingerprints on my life, learning to trust Him

again. However, that trust didn't begin through dramatic epi-
sodes like His grace shown to me at the time of Barbara's death.
It began by believing Him for a simple thing like an empty parking space at the employment office. And later, by seeing His
hand in my getting a job with the only two airlines in the world to
whom I had not applied.

3
The Empty Parking Space

If ye have faith as a grain of mustard seed, ye shall say unto this mountain, Remove hence to yonder place; and it shall remove; and nothing shall be impossible unto you (Matt. 17:20, KJV).

Many years passed, and I was a young adult before I allowed myself to think once more of that personal God I'd known as a child. However, the day did come when I was challenged again to return to that childlike faith. A friend had given me a book called *Think and Grow Rich* by Napoleon Hill. It contained a collection of stories about successful people. The thing that was so fascinating to me was the common theme that ran throughout each story. Every person mentioned in the book spoke of a positive mental attitude and a faith in the power of prayer. For me the book was far more than a "get-out-there-and-go-for-it" instruction manual. It asked the reader to step out in faith—to not only pray for needs but to pray specifically—and to believe the thing we prayed for would come to pass.

My dream had always been to become an airline pilot. At the time, I was a flight instructor for light airplanes at Carpenter's Airport in Charlotte. I was grateful for having come that far, but it seemed like an awfully long way to my ultimate dream. While sitting at the airport one day waiting for my next student, I thumbed through my dog-eared copy of *Think and Grow Rich*. As always, I was captivated by the author's presentation. Was he crazy? Or could what I was reading really work? Of course, I still believed in God, but I didn't really think He concerned Himself about my individual problems and dreams. After all, He had some genuinely big problems in the world that needed solving without worrying about the small daily demands of my life.

Yet, the assertion of Napoleon Hill's book that God does answer specific prayers was gnawing at me. What I wanted more than anything was to become an airline pilot, but I was afraid to even let myself think about God helping me become one—much less pray specifically for it. I still remembered the pain of His letting me lose Dad; at least, in my heart I blamed Him for that. But as I permitted myself to dream just a little, a thought occurred to me. Maybe I couldn't believe for an airline job, but I could start by believing for something small—something not quite so essential to my life's dream.

There was one thing that had been bugging me—something small, yet something that had become very irritating. Charlotte's job as a tax consultant had played out with the end of tax season. She had been signing up every Tuesday for her unemployment check. Since we only had one car, I had to drive her to the employment office every week. The irritating part of the ordeal was that the place was so busy on sign-up day that I usually had to park at least two or three blocks away. I slammed the book shut and sat up straight. "That's it," I said to myself. "That's the perfect place to start."

"OK," I said, now directing my words to God. "I'm going to accept Mr. Hill's challenge." I tried to make my voice sound firm with confidence. "I'm asking You for an empty parking space right in front of the employment office: the first one to the right of the handicap spaces." I wanted to be absolutely sure if the experiment did work that there would be no doubt left in my mind. If that particular space was empty, it could not be a coincidence!

It was almost a week before the next sign-up Tuesday, and every day I would remind God of the parking space I wished to be empty. Every day I would tell myself, "I believe that the first parking space to the right of the handicap space will be vacant."

It was a few days before I found the nerve to tell Charlotte. "Oh, sure," she said laughing. "You actually expect that exact parking space to be empty."

"You'll see." I said, trying to sound more confident than I felt.

Finally the day arrived. We lived in a house trailer on the airport property, so I waited until after my morning training flight to pick up Charlotte. I knew that would put us at the employment office during the busiest part of the day. If it worked, I wanted to be sure it was God who did it. It was about 10:30 a.m. when I drove over to our trailer and honked the horn to let her know I was ready to go.

Soon she was sliding into the seat next to me with her purse tucked under her arm, trying her best to act as usual, but she couldn't quite hide the sly grin that kept popping out. I backed out of the drive and headed toward downtown Charlotte—and my rendezvous with God. Charlotte had to keep cautioning me to slow down. I was in a hurry by then to see if it was going to work. But halfway there, I got scared. What was I doing? This was not something to play around with. *What if it really did work?* My next thought was: *But on the other hand, what will I do if it doesn't work?* I knew it'd be hard to handle the disappointment.

Charlotte had stopped teasing me and sat very still looking quietly out her window. "O. A.," she said, her voice serious this time. "Do you really think it'll be empty?"

"Yes, I do," I confessed, surprising myself at my own firm response. Even more surprising was the confidence that suddenly began welling up inside me.

Soon I was turning into the front parking lot, and confidence or no confidence, my hair practically stood on end when I saw a car slowly backing out of my exact designated parking space as we approached. I couldn't get a word out. Charlotte sat there staring at the empty space, her laughter and "I told you so" suspended in midair. Neither of us moved at first. Then we started beating each other on the shoulders, laughing, and talking at the same time. Even after I'd parked, it took several minutes for us to compose ourselves enough for her to get out of the car and go in.

I watched her walk toward the office and turn again to stare at the packed parking lot. Some cars were even parked illegally. And she was still shaking her head when she disappeared through the office doors.

I smiled as the doors closed behind her and slumped silently back in my seat. I was alone with my thoughts, but at the same time, I wasn't alone. All of a sudden, I was sharply aware of His presence—the same awareness I remembered feeling as a child when somehow I just knew He was there. I could even imagine the smile He must have had as He watched me. I was still a long way from the daily carefree confidence I had once known, but I knew I had finally taken a big step in that direction.

The miracle for Charlotte and me was far more than just finding an empty parking space. It meant endless possibilities lay ahead for us if we could learn to follow up on what we had learned that day—trust and believe. Today, it was a parking space—perhaps tomorrow—an airline job.

4

Up, Up, and Away

Therefore do not worry about tomorrow, for tomorrow will worry about itself. Each day has enough trouble of its own (Matt. 6:34).

Until I was seventeen, I had given very little thought to airplanes or flying, but that was about to change. After Daddy died, money became scarce at our house. I couldn't find a job; so as a last resort, I talked Mama into signing for me to join the Air Force. My first airplane ride came when I boarded an Eastern Airlines Super Constellation to fly from Charlotte to San Antonio, Texas, where I was to undergo basic training.

As we sat at the end of the runway at the Charlotte airport, and the pilot began to rev the four powerful, propellor-driven engines, I immediately was hooked on flying. A thrill shot through me like I'd never felt before. And, suddenly, we were hurtling down the runway with the world rushing past my window so fast I could hardly get my breath. Then we broke ground and gently floated into a world I'd never imagined, but one I definitely knew I had to become a part of someday.

Any hopes of flying for the Air Force were dashed to pieces because I hadn't finished high school, but as soon as I was discharged, I returned to school with the aid of the GI Bill. I also started visiting the local airport which consisted of a single dirt landing strip and an old wooden hangar. With encouragement from Hubert Lancaster, our only local flight instructor, I began flying lessons. On June 18, 1953, I made my first two solo take-offs and landings. Jack Matheny, another student pilot, and I became co-owners of a 1946 Piper Cub which we purchased for $500.

I earned my student pilot's license and high school diploma, but I was still uncertain about my direction and future. The provisions for education in the GI Bill were used up for me. I had no money for college, and I was barely making a living at my textile job. Becoming an airline pilot seemed impossible, but I felt deep down inside I had to be in aviation.

After a few agonizing months, an opportunity for a job in Buffalo, New York, came through my brother, Eugene, and I took it. It involved working for a subsidiary of Chevrolet delivering engines for military transport planes, during the Korean War. Sadly, this meant I had to sell my half of the Cub to Jack.

My salary at Chevrolet enabled me to save enough money in one year to enter Spartan School of Aeronautics in Tulsa, Oklahoma, where I would earn an aircraft mechanic's license. I also worked evenings at the local Douglas Aircraft plant. This enabled me to earn enough money to continue my flying lessons on weekends at Tulsa's Harvey Young Airport. And by the time I finished the Spartan mechanic's school, I had also earned my private pilot's license.

When I went back to Buffalo, I married Charlotte, the sweetheart I'd left behind. I then started working with Bell Aircraft and took a part-time mechanic's job with Niagara Airways's fixed-based operator at the Niagara Falls Airport. An agreement with the company allowed me a cheap rate for renting their aircraft which enabled me to quickly earn enough hours to receive my Commercial License, Flight Instructor's Rating, and an Instrument Rating.

It seemed as though things were working out at last. Instead of having to pay to fly, I was finally being paid to fly sightseers over Niagara Falls and teach others to fly. All this was in addition, of course, to my full-time job at Bell Aircraft.

But it wasn't long before Bell's government contract expired, and I found myself without a full-time job. The part-time flying job at Niagara Airways wasn't sufficient to support my family. Fortunately, however, an offer did come from a new Douglas Aircraft plant that had recently located in Charlotte, North Carolina; so I loaded up Charlotte, my wife, and Barbara, our new baby, and moved south.

As soon as I became established at Douglas, I scouted out the local airports and landed a part-time flight instructor's job at Carpenter's Airport. I also enrolled in night courses at the University of North Carolina at Charlotte. About this time, our second daughter, Cheryl, was born.

The next couple of years were like walking a tightrope, trying to juggle two jobs, my home life, and college. With only a faint hope of becoming an airline pilot and taking a drastic cut in pay, I left Douglas and began flying full-time out of Carpenter Airport. That's where I was the day my friend gave me *Think and Grow Rich* by Napoleon Hill. I didn't know it, but it was time for God to put into action the next phase of His plan for my life. After the parking-space miracle, I felt inspired to actively pursue an airline career. I wanted it so badly I could taste it. I dreamed constantly of having the controls of a giant airliner responding to my touch, so I spent plenty in postage stamps writing to every airline in the world, inquiring about their pilot needs. Every airline, that is, except Eastern Airlines and Mohawk, a regional airline in the northeast later bought by another carrier. Eastern was my first choice, but they had laid off hundreds of pilots, and I felt it would be a waste of time to write them. I didn't write to Mohawk either.

Only four or five airlines bothered to answer my letter, and only two of those included applications in their reply. Accompanying the applications were notes which, in essence, read, "You can fill these out if you'd like, but you'll just be wasting your time."

I was discouraged, but remembering the empty-parking-space miracle kept me from giving up. Later I heard that a major airline was interviewing prospective pilots in Atlanta, Georgia. So I loaded up my family before dawn the next morning and headed for Atlanta.

The interviewing process dragged on until about ten o'clock that night. It was a hot, grueling day for Charlotte and the girls. They spent the whole time with our car in a paid parking lot. Charlotte even had to wash the girls in the bathroom sink. But she was happy when it was over, because she knew I was hopeful. The interviewer had all but promised me a job. He said I would be receiving an airline ticket within seven days to fly to Washington, D.C., for further evaluation and a physical.

So every day the next week, I waited anxiously for the mail carrier. But there was no letter. On the eighth day, I called the gentleman who had interviewed me and heard these dreaded words: "Sorry, but the training class was filled before we got down to your name." My hopes and dreams were devastated by that call. A nauseous feeling began to consume me.

The next Sunday, Charlotte talked me into visiting a newly founded Presbyterian Church with her and the girls. In my zeal to build flying time, I seldom attended church except on bad weather weekends, but in spite of a beautiful, sunny day that Sunday, I was in church with my family.

It was a friendly country church. Charlie, one of my flight students, had invited us. He couldn't wait to introduce me to "Red" Guthrie, an Eastern captain friend of his. As we shook hands, Red looked at me sympathetically.

"Hear you just got turned down by (so and so)," he said. "Best thing that ever happened to you."

"Wha . . . what?" I sputtered. Didn't he know how badly I was hurting inside? I didn't understand his words or particularly appreciate his comment that morning. After all, surely he of all people knew the scarcity of airline pilot jobs. There wasn't the luxury of being able to choose an airline. I was simply hoping for a job.

"Tell me something, O. A.," he said. "Who do you really want to fly for?"

"Well, Eastern, of course," I gasped, "but that's impossible. They have hundreds of pilots on furlough."

"Same thing happened to me," Red went on as though he hadn't heard a word I was saying. "I was turned down by the same airline that turned you down, and six months later I was working for Eastern."

"But, but," I tried to interrupt.

"And the same thing's going to happen to you," Red assured with a smile, patting me on the shoulder as he walked away. Years later when we had become old airline buddies, I discovered I had been talking to a real man of faith that day.

Shortly after meeting Red, God brought another Eastern captain my way. His name was John Clower, the assistant chief pilot of the Charlotte base. He came to Carpenter's Airport one day and asked to have his flying skills checked out in a Champion Tri-Traveler—a small tandem, two-seater, stick-controlled plane. John hadn't flown light airplanes in years and wanted to teach his son to fly. We hit it off from the start, and he seemed genuinely interested when I shared with him my dream of someday becoming an airline pilot.

However, it turned out that the combined weight of John and his strapping, teenage son was too heavy for our Tri-Traveler, so he had to go elsewhere and find a larger trainer plane. After that, we lost contact for a while.

Later, in order to further my flying experience, I left Carpenter's to fly for Cannon Aircraft, located in Charlotte's Municipal Airport. One day, I received a surprise call from John. Yet, I guess it shouldn't have been a surprise because it happened exactly six months after Red's prophecy that Sunday morning at the Presbyterian church.

"Hello. Is this O. A.?" the voice said.

"Yes, it is," I replied.

"Well, this is John Clower. "How would you like to come to work for Eastern?" he said.

I could hardly keep my voice steady; I had waited so long. "Well, I, uh, yes. I'd like that," I stammered.

"Maybe you could drive over here, and we could talk," he suggested.

It was about two miles around the airport perimeter road, but before John could hardly cradle his phone, I was standing in his office. After greeting me with a broad smile, he explained that telegrams were being sent out to recall all the furloughed Eastern pilots and two classes of new hirings were being planned for the following February. (This was in the fall of 1961.) He also reported that Captain O. B. Bivens, an old friend of his, would be doing the interviewing.

"How would you like for me to give O. B. a call?" John asked from behind his big oak desk. My mouth felt as if it were stuffed with cotton. He just chuckled, waved at me as if to say you're hopeless, laid down his pencil, and finally picked up his phone. "O. B., John Clower here," he said. "I've got a young man here who I believe will make us one heck of a pilot." He winked at me.

Finally after further conversation, John put his hand over the phone and leaned toward me: "He wants to know if you can come down tonight for an interview tomorrow morning." He looked at his watch, grabbed a flight schedule from his desk, and continued: "Can you be packed and back here ready to go in an hour?"

My mind was racing—*if I call Charlotte and ask her to pack my bags, it's a ten-minute drive each way.* "Sure I can!"

Speaking to O. B. again, John said, "He'll be there." Hanging up, John said, "Better get going! I'll have some instructions written out for you by the time you get back."

I immediately called Cannon Aircraft to let them know I needed the afternoon and the next day off. Barbara, the secretary who answered, became almost as excited as I when I shared my story, and she agreed to call Charlotte about packing my bags. When I arrived at the trailer, I didn't have time to talk. I grabbed my bags, kissed her, and bolted out the door for the airport. I made it with only minutes to spare.

The flight to Miami and my stay at the hotel across the street from the Eastern training base was like a dream. I could hardly believe it: Eastern, the one airline I had wanted to fly for all the time, and I was here.

The next morning at 8:30 sharp, I was ushered into Captain Bivens's office. Fortunately, he had the same easygoing, friendly manner as John Clower, and he put me at ease immediately. The interview went well, and soon I was facing a barrage of written exams and a thorough physical examination. When I finished I stuck my head back into Captain Bivens' office as he had requested me to do. "We'll let you know something as soon as we can," he said.

Then it was back home to wait—again. In the beginning, I'd call John Clower about once a week to check on any progress. Then I'd call him about every other day, and then it became every day. I'd call John, and he'd call O. B. This continued for about two months, until finally O. B. reported to John, "Tell O.

A. not to call anymore. I've filled the first class with pilots laid off from other airlines, but I'll definitely have him in the second class starting in February." I was thrilled, but I still didn't rest easy until the official notification arrived in the mail several weeks later. That letter was mounted and hangs on my wall today.

On February 12, 1962, I became an Eastern pilot. *The end of my rainbow,* or so I thought. Then came ground school, flight training, tests, and flight checks. Two months later, I was qualified as copilot on Convair 440s and Martin 404s, twin-engine, propellor-driven airplanes carrying between forty to fifty passengers. My first flight was a fantasy come true.

Just two months after this I couldn't believe it, when the Eastern flight engineers walked out on strike, the airline shut down, and my bubble burst.

Charlotte and I still had the house trailer, and it was paid for, but there was not even enough money in the bank to buy groceries. We knew we had to take emergency measures, and since it appeared that the strike was going to be long, we decided to visit her folks in Buffalo.

I helped her dad with his floor-covering business, hoping for a speedy strike settlement. Since Eastern didn't fly into Buffalo at that time, nothing about the strike was in the news. After several weeks, I made a call to John Clower to get an update.

"No, things still look pretty bad," he gloomily replied. "But it's strange you called now. Mohawk Airlines, down in Utica, New York, just called to see if we could furnish them some dual-trained Convair and Martin copilots. They need about twelve pilots, but I have about twenty here in the office wanting the job. We're going to draw straws." He was gone for a minute, and then he was back, "Hey, the guys say I can draw one for you."

I was among those chosen, and early the next morning I flew from Buffalo to Utica, New York, where I underwent a half-day refresher course. By that mid-afternoon, I was out of Utica as copilot on a Martin 404 passenger flight. I continued to fly for Mohawk until Eastern started flying again in the fall of '62.

Was it simply a coincidence that I ended up flying for the only two airlines to whom I had not applied? There was no way I could be convinced of that. I am certain it was God letting me know that He held my tomorrows, and all He wants is for me to hold firmly to Him.

5

How God Turned My Heart Toward His Word

Teach me, O Lord, to follow your decrees;
then I will keep them to the end.
Give me understanding, and I will keep your law
and obey it with all my heart.
Direct me in the path of your commands,
for there I find delight.
Turn my heart toward your statutes
and not toward selfish gain.
Turn my eyes away from worthless things;
renew my life according to your word (Ps. 119:33-37).

I was twenty-seven—almost twenty-eight—years old when I was hired by Eastern Airlines. And suddenly, the struggle I'd lived with for all those years was gone. My dream had come true. I'd reached the impossible goal, and I for some reason found myself thinking, now what? It should have been time for the happily-ever-after ending to begin, but for some reason, it wasn't working out that way.

During the fall of 1962, Eastern was able to get back into operation from the flight engineer strike, but only on a limited basis. Most of the engineers refused to come back; at that time, the Railway Labor Act did not permit the company to hire strikebreakers from outside. They were able to get around this by taking their bottom 272 pilots and training them to be flight engineers. I was next to the bottom number on this list. And our copilot seats were filled with new-hires. So not only did I have to fly engineer, but I was also transferred from out of our beloved Charlotte to Boston in the dead of the winter. As an engineer, I was initially qualified on DC 7's and Constellations, then later on Lockheed Electras. An important role of the flight engineer is performing a thorough preflight check, and it was no picnic pre-flighting airplanes on the Boston International Airport tarmac with blistering winter winds whistling in off Boston Harbor. I was mostly assigned to the backup airplanes for the Boston to New York Shuttle, and many days I would preflight as many as six airplanes in a day. I remember once muttering under my breath while kicking the tires of an old Super Constellation, wondering if it could be the same airplane I had taken my first airplane ride on ten years earlier—the one that had infected me with the "flying bug."

It did help some after a couple of years, when I managed to get based at the Washington National Airport. I was glad to get a little further south, but I knew it would be at least another year before I'd get to fly copilot again, and I sure missed it.

My seniority number was such that all I could hold at that time was a reserve line which meant sitting around home a lot waiting for a call out. When on reserve, except for the ten days a month we were scheduled off, we were on call twenty-four hours a day. All that sitting around and not knowing day or night when I might get suddenly called began driving me stir crazy. For a little while, Charlotte seemed to enjoy my being home. For the first time in our married life, we were able to spend time together, but pretty soon she wasn't so sure it was a good idea anymore. I was becoming increasingly edgy. I was also depressed over not feeling productive. In the past, my goals had always driven me to a high degree of accomplishment, but suddenly, it seemed that I was going nowhere. I had just turned thirty, and I felt my life had crested; there was nowhere to go but down, and I couldn't seem to stop the plunge. Soon I could tell that Charlotte was even getting a bit concerned about my state of mind.

In reality, everything should have been great. We lived in a comfortable home in the Virginia suburbs; we were attending Faith United Methodist Church a few blocks from our home; and Phil Hunsicker, the young pastor, was one of my best friends. We had a lovely family. Our third daughter, Lisa, who was born in New Hampshire where we lived while being based in Boston, was three years old, and our fourth daughter, Kim, was on the way. Even with all the bad points of my engineer's job, it would still have to be considered among the best jobs in the airline industry. So I had a loving family, a good church, great friends, and a promising airline career, yet something was missing. I couldn't understand why I was feeling so lousy, and nothing I did seemed to help.

One night I lay in bed, thinking about my life when, without warning, everything caved in. I began crying—not gentle, quiet tears, but harsh, loud sobbing. It seemed as though there was a tearing apart of my soul somewhere deep inside. Any other time, any noise—any sound from the girls or me— would wake Charlotte, but that night, I somehow feel God had put her into a sound sleep so He could recreate me—much like He had put Adam to sleep when He took from Adam's side a rib to create Eve.

"God," I begged. "If I'm going to live a Christian life, a real Christian life, You're going to have to do something. You're going to have to take over. I've tried, and all I do is mess up. Nothing seems to satisfy. God, if being a Christian doesn't work in everyday life, then I don't want any part of it. It can't be real. I give up. I'm throwing the ball in Your court, Lord. It's up to You now."

Finally, I'd gotten desperate enough to get honest with God; strangely enough, after I had, a peace came over me, and I fell sound asleep—the most restful sleep that I had enjoyed in a long time.

The next morning I felt embarrassed about what had happened, too embarrassed even to tell Charlotte. I was just glad she hadn't woke up. I tried to convince myself I'd just had another emotional experience; I had just lost my cool, and nothing would come of it. But before I could even finish eating breakfast, something did. I suddenly realized a consuming desire to get to know God—to learn everything the Bible had to say about Him. Since the power of God is supernatural, and the Holy Spirit lives in us, it was a supernatural desire—not a passing fantasy but a desire that has never left me.

As soon as I finished breakfast, I grabbed a Bible and curled up in my easy chair in the living room. I read all day that day, the next day, and the next. Charlotte became concerned that I had become some sort of a religious fanatic. I guess she was partly right. I was a fanatic about wanting to know God through His Word. She had to run me from chair to chair with the vacuum cleaner in order to get the house clean. In moments of frustration, she would say, "How can you sit there and read that Book all day long?"

But she didn't understand at that time what I was getting out of the reading. Not only was I learning who God was, but I was also learning who I was and how I related to Him and to fellow human beings through Christ Jesus. I was comforted to discover that the apostle Paul talked about experiencing the same sort of struggle that I had been encountering, because he wrote in Romans 7:18-19: "I know that nothing good lives in me, that is, in my sinful nature. For I have the desire to do what is good, but I cannot carry it out. For what I do is not the good I want to do; no, the evil I do not want to do—this I keep on doing." And in his frustration, Paul also cried out (v. 24), "What a wretched man I am! Who will rescue me from this body of death?" He concluded in verse 25, "Thanks be to God—through Jesus Christ our Lord!" I became more enlightened on the solution to my problem through Jesus' own words. "If you hold to my teaching, you are really my disciples. Then you will know the truth, and the truth will set you free" (John 8:31-32). In fact, I discovered that these words were true.

The more I read and put into practice the things I read, the more freedom I enjoyed in my spirit—freedom such as peace, joy, faith, hope, and love. I discovered that the Word of God truly was the food of the spirit: The food for which I hungered. I found as the days passed that it was a hunger that could never be quite satisfied—a goal, unlike the others I had sought, that I could never quite reach and would continue through the years to challenge my faith and relationship to God, His church, and my fellow human beings.

6
Answer to My Writer's Prayer

Ask and it will be given to you; seek and you will find; knock and the door will be opened to you. For everyone who asks receives; he who seeks finds; and to him who knocks, the door will be opened (Luke 11:9-10).

The more I read the Bible, the more excited I became. Not only did I experience a remarkable change in my character and attitude over time, but I also discovered principles and concepts that brought forth incredible results when I followed them.

I was attending an Adult Sunday School class at Faith United Methodist Church at that time. I enjoyed the meetings very much. The discussions were stimulating because most of the members were as hungry as I was to know about the the things of God. The only problem was that I was so shy and inhibited when it came to talking about God that I wasn't able to take an active part in the discussions. My feelings on the subject were so strong that I was afraid of losing control of my emotions—afraid of crying. Even though I would be dying to share my own insights on the lesson being discussed, because of that fear, I'd just sit there and play dumb. If I was called on to read more than one verse of Scripture—or more than I could read with one breath—I would almost pass out. So although I loved the class, most of the time I went home totally frustrated.

It had always been much easier for me to express myself through writing, and a number of teachers had told me over the years that I had a flair for putting words on paper, complimenting me on subject papers that I handed in. But during high school and beyond, interest in English and other liberal arts courses gave way to such basic things as earning a living and taking care of my family, plus my obsession with flying. So I was left with a gap in my education, a limited vocabulary, very little spelling skills, and no idea where to place commas—all very essential parts of writing. Yet that secret desire to write was always there, just beneath the surface.

My inability to vocalize my thoughts and feelings concerning God seemed to bring my need to write even closer to the front—so much so, that I made it a focal point of my prayers. I wrestled with the problem and sought God's guidance until one day the need for an answer came to a boiling point. I was stuck in heavy traffic trying to get from my Alexander home to the Washington National Airport. "God," I said, "You gave Gideon his answer using a fleece. Why can't You give me a sign for my answer. Am I supposed to be a writer or not?"

This question had no sooner left my lips when I had a sudden impulse to turn on my car radio, which was strange because I seldom listened to the radio. I merely reached over and flicked on the knob without touching the dial. Suddenly the announcer was saying in a strong, clear voice, "The written word is still the most effective and powerful form of communication!"

"Wow!" I exclaimed and immediately turned the radio off. I never knew or even wondered about the context of the announcer's speech. I only knew that I had asked God for an answer, and He had given me one.

Unfortunately, I interpreted this sign to mean I was to become a writer right away. After all, I'd been doing what God wanted and sharing my insights of the Scriptures on paper without having to actually "talk" to people at all seemed like the answer. A few days later I sent for information about a writer's correspondence course. Within a few weeks, a sales representative for the school was knocking at my door. After being invited in, he immediately began complimenting me on the results of my aptitude test. I was really flying high until he told me the price of the course. My copilot's salary provided for my family a comfortable living, but there was little left over for extras. I excused myself long enough to discuss the idea with Charlotte. All she said was, "Honey, do you really think we can afford it at this time?"

But when the salesman heard her comment, he took offense

and became very rude. "This is your husband's decision," he said. "I think you should leave the matter entirely up to him." His sudden arrogance made me so angry that before I knew it, I'd forgotten all about writing and was tossing him out of my house.

I sat there later that night thinking about the whole situation. Had I missed God's intention? If so, what was He trying to tell me? After a period of seeking, He began to show me my error in thinking. My motive for writing was to escape having to face up to my inability to verbalize my innermost thoughts and feelings. Yes, God wanted me to write, but in His timing. However, my inhibition was a problem that would have to be dealt with first.

I had asked, I had sought, I had knocked, and I had received an answer—not the one I wanted—but still God's answer.

7

Miracle Land

The Lord had said to Abram, "Leave your country, your people and your father's household and go to the land I will show you" (Gen. 12:1).

Having grown up in the lengthening shadows of the Blue Ridge Mountains in North Carolina, I was never content living anywhere else. To me, there is a spiritual quality about those mountains which speaks of strength, stability, courage, and endurance. My longing to return home was always present.

I was grateful to have been living as far south as Washington, D.C., but that wasn't close enough. The best base for me was Atlanta, but there was a problem of my lack of seniority. Washington was a more "junior" base. Consequently, it was where I could check out as Captain at the earliest time. Holding a captain's slot in Atlanta seemed light years away, yet I knew when I did eventually make it, a commute from there to North Carolina would be easy. There were daily flights between Charlotte and Atlanta and Greenville-Spartanburg and Atlanta. I wanted to be located somewhere in that area.

I had asked my Uncle Frank and Aunt Eddie, who lived in the region, to be on the lookout for property for sale. I was visiting them in the summer of 1967 when the story began to unfold. They lived in a small, wooden-frame tenant house located on some of the most beautiful acreage I'd ever seen. It was filled with rolling pasture land, hardwood and pine forests, and two bubbling mountain streams. Uncle Frank and I were talking and rocking on their front porch. It was relaxing sitting there watching Uncle Frank and listening to a little brook dance across the pasture.

"Well, Uncle Frank," I asked, "have you found any land for sale yet?"

"Nope," he answered, stroking the two-day-old stubble on his chin. He thought for a moment and then continued, "You know, Dee, that is, Mr. Harrill who owns this place, just might be in the notion to sell."

I brought my rocking chair to a screeching halt, and I leaned forward in rapt attention. "What makes you say that?" I asked, trying to sound casual, but inside I was screaming, *This place . . . for sale! Mercy, I'd love to own this land!*

"Well, he had a man out here looking yesterday," Uncle Frank continued. "And I'm sure he was trying to buy this old place."

"What about Dee? Did he sound interested?" I asked.

"Don't rightly know," mused Uncle Frank. "I heard the man offer him $12,000, and Dee just sorta shook his head and grinned. But I'm thinking, maybe, if you was to offer him . . . say fourteen . . ."

"Fourteen thousand!" I exclaimed. "Surely you're kidding. There's no way that he would sell for that." There were eighty-seven acres of land, Frank's little house, and another unoccupied farmhouse that Dee used for storage. There was also a large barn, thirty acres of fenced-in pasture, and a large tract of timber. Because it was located at a crossroads, there was close to a mile of road frontage.

I'd never had the opportunity to look over the property, but with only a hint from me, Uncle Frank grabbed his old panama hat, and we were ready to go. We jumped in my old Dodge runabout and started up the road. As we passed the vacant farmhouse, Frank shouted, "Well, how about that? There's Dee now!" I wheeled into the driveway where Frank was pointing and spotted the tall, frail-looking old gentleman sitting on a stool as he tended his vegetable garden. We shook hands as Frank introduced us. I hoped he wouldn't notice my sweaty palms or the fact that I could hardly contain myself. After a few minutes, I blurted out, "Mr. Harrill, Frank here tells me you might consider selling this place."

Harrill looked me up and down slowly, took off his hat, swatted at some flies, kicked the plowed dirt with his brogans, and answered, "Don't know. You interested?"

"Yes sir," I replied nervously but enthusiastically.

Then, without blinking, he stared me straight in the eyes. "What'd you want it for?"

"Well, I'd like to fix it up, build me a house, and someday retire here," I said.

"You wouldn't come in and cut down all the trees, would you?" he asked with a frown.

"No Sir! Not in a million years. That would be the last thing I'd want to do." I could sense Harrill's deep love for the place, and it touched me. Dee lived in town, but he still drove out almost every day to tend his garden and putter around. And he charged my aunt and uncle very little rent. He liked having them around to help look after the place.

Harrill looked down at the ground, out over the pasture, and then up toward the mountain on the north side of the property. Finally, after what seemed an eternity, he remarked, "I like you. If you'll do like you promise and take care of the place, you can have it for twelve thousand." My legs turned to rubber. I squatted down and doodled in the dirt with my finger, hoping he wouldn't notice my tears. This was beyond my wildest dreams. Even on copilot's pay, I could swing it. Finally I gained control of my emotions, swallowed hard, and said, "I'll take it, and I promise you that you won't be sorry you sold it to me."

"How do you plan on paying for it?" he asked.

"Well, I've got three thousand saved, and I think I can get the rest financed," I told him.

"How about if I carry the mortgage for you at six percent?" he asked.

"Sure," I said, "that would be fine." I was still having a hard time believing this was happening.

"How long will you give me to get rid of all my stuff? It's spread all over the place," Harrill asked.

I said, "Take as long as you like. As a matter-of-fact, I'd like to see you continue putting your garden in for as long as you like.

Besides, it'll probably be several years before I can build a house and move down."

Harrill's smile spread from ear to ear as he poked out his hand, and I reached mine forward. "It's a deal!" he said. It was more than that to me—it was a miracle. I didn't understand the full scope of the occurrence until God revealed it to me sometime later.

8

My City Wife Becomes a Country Girl

Therefore, if anyone is in Christ, he is a new creation; the old has gone, the new has come! (2 Cor. 5:17).

Charlotte had stayed with Aunt Eddie while Frank and I had gone to check out the property. I could just imagine how excited those two would be when we got back and told them about the deal.

"Hey, Hon!" I shouted as we burst through the front screen door. "Guess what?" But there was no answer, and about the time I said, "Hey Hon" again, Aunt Eddie came out of the kitchen wiping her hands on her apron. "Guess what, Aunt Eddie. I'm buying the property! I'm buying this place from Dee!"

"Well boys, that's good news," she said, using one of her familiar expressions.

"Where's Charlotte?" I asked.

With a grin she nodded toward their spare bedroom door. I looked in and there she was sound asleep across Aunt Eddie's feather-tick bed. I ran in and shook her awake. "Guess what? Guess what?" I said grinning with excitement. *She's going to love it,* I kept thinking to myself.

"Wha. . . what's happening?" She asked, as she sat up on the bed trying to rub the sleep out of her eyes.

"Well, we're going to buy this property—this beautiful property—for twelve thousand dollars! That's what's happening!" I sat back with a pleased expression on my face.

"We're what!" she said, suddenly coming wide awake.

"I said, 'I just bought this property, this property right

here,' " I emphasized pointing to the floor, "for twelve thousand dollars." But her face registered anything but joy.

"You've put us in debt for twelve thousand dollars!" she exclaimed.

"You don't understand," I protested. "This place has got to be worth at least thirty thousand dollars."

"What are you going do with it?" she asked, but before I could answer, she continued, "We certainly live too far away to come down here regularly. I just don't . . ."

As she went on, a sick feeling gathered in the pit of my stomach. "Well, I was hoping someday we might build a home right here," I offered.

"Are you crazy!" She was almost shouting at me by this time. "Well, you're sure not going to get me to live in the country!"

I realized then I was in trouble. Charlotte had lived in New York City until she was seven, then moved to Buffalo where she lived until we were married. When we left Buffalo, we moved to Charlotte, then to Exeter, a small town in New Hampshire where we lived for a short while, and then it was on to the suburb of D.C. She had never lived in the country, and, evidently, she had no desire to even try it.

I was heartsick over the situation. In fact, I might have backed out because of the strain I knew it was going to put on our marriage. But there was a deep feeling, that for some reason, God wanted me to buy the property. I certainly couldn't explain it, I didn't know why myself. And all I could do was pray that Charlotte would somehow have a change of heart.

I was finally able to convince Charlotte that we should buy the property. But I knew she didn't like the idea any more than she had at first; she was just going along with me because she knew I wanted it so badly. After we'd made the purchase I began flying down on my days off and using it to get away. To make it handy, I even kept my old Dodge runabout parked at the Charlotte Airport. Of course, those visits used up my off days with the family and gave Charlotte another excuse to dislike the property. "God," I kept asking, "how can she hate something that I love so much?"

Just getting away from the city and the pressure of my job was rejuvenating to me—to visit with Frank and Eddie and enjoy their relaxed lifestyle, to wade in the streams and catch tadpoles, to hike through the woods, or sometimes just to find a grassy spot and lie on my back dreaming of my boyhood days on the farm or the camping trips we used to make to the Smokey Mountains.

Months went by, and after what seemed like an agonizingly long time, God began to change my wife's thinking. It began by Charlotte getting interested in girl scouts. I came home one day from a flight and found a lady having coffee with her. It turned out that this woman was in charge of girl scouts throughout the D.C. area, and before Charlotte finished introducing us, she reached out to shake my hand. "Congratulations," she said, "your wife has just volunteered to be a girl scout leader and organizer. She's going to help us get at least five troops going in this area.

I was thrilled surprised but thrilled. "What's this all about?" I said, directing my question to Charlotte.

"Well," she began, "Barbara wants to be a girl scout. You know how much she enjoyed being a Brownie in New Hampshire, but there's not one girl scout troop in this whole area for her to join. So I'm going to change that."

Organizing was something that Charlotte loved. Everywhere we had lived, she'd wasted no time getting involved in the community, the schools, and the church. And if she saw something that needed attention, she'd either join a committee or form a committee and go to work on it. Before long there was girl scout paraphernalia lying around our house: uniform pieces, instruction manuals, first-aid kits, camping gear, and hundreds of boxes of girl scout cookies. But what really surprised me was around January of that year, when Charlotte announced that she and her new leaders were going camping.

"Oh, you mean when it gets to be warm weather," I said.

"Well, the end of March," she said, "we're going up in the Blue Ridge Mountains."

"But it's still wintry in the mountains at that time of year!" I told her.

"I don't care. That's the only time we can do it in order to be qualified to take our girls camping this summer," she explained.

And, go they did. It was on Friday when they left, and they planned on coming home Monday. Charlotte was almost six months pregnant with our fourth daughter, Kim, and a late winter storm dumped four inches of snow on them just after they arrived at camp. I was off that weekend and gladly agreed, along with the help of a neighbor, to look after Barbara, Cheryl, and Lisa while Charlotte was gone. But I was praying the whole weekend, afraid that Charlotte had made a mistake in going. I just knew she was going to come back hating the out-of-doors after the weekend. After all, no one could enjoy camping in the weather they were having. I dreaded to see her arrive home.

But when she did, I couldn't believe my eyes or ears. The girl that came bouncing through our front door that Monday afternoon didn't even resemble my wife. Oh, she looked like Charlotte. She was dressed like Charlotte, but she didn't act like Charlotte. She was filled with exuberance and couldn't talk for giggling. "You're not going to believe it!" she kept saying. "It was absolutely gorgeous up there. There was snow all over the place; the trees were just hanging with it."

"But where did you sleep?" I asked, beginning to catch her enthusiasm, but curious to know how they had survived.

"In a big, log cabin with a fireplace at one end," she started giggling again, "and there was no wood. We had a heck of a time finding wood. There was just one light bulb hanging down from the center of the ceiling, and we had to use an outside toilet. We even had to cook outside because there weren't any kitchen facilities."

"And you enjoyed that?" I laughed incredulously. The whole thing was throwing me.

"We all had to sleep next to the fireplace to keep warm," Charlotte said, still giggling, "and we all stunk to high heavens. It was a ball!" At that, she just started rolling with laughter. That was only the beginning.

For the next several summers, Charlotte lived and breathed girl scout camping. Even after Kim was born and still an infant, she would load the baby in her basket and take her with them.

Suddenly, she loved roughing it, sleeping in tents, cooking over an open campfire, and bathing in lakes and streams. She learned to do it all, and I was tickled to death. But what delighted me most was the affection she had developed for the out-of-doors. Soon she was even dropping hints that she might enjoy living in the country after all.

Besides her involvement with scouting, Charlotte became more active in the church and was showing an increased interest in spiritual things. She was reading her Bible more and attending home prayer meetings and Bible studies. She had also started going to a Monday night church service which she called "Church of Northern Virginia." This commenced about the same time a couple from Oklahoma began attending our church. They had come from an Assembly of God background, and I suspected maybe they were Pentecostal and maybe the meetings Charlotte was attending were Pentecostal, but that didn't bother me. I liked my new wife.

It was apparent that God was at work in both of our lives, forming us into new creations. I didn't understand all that was happening, but I could see the fingerprints of God sticking out all over it.

9

The Call

Jesus called the children to him and said, "Let the little children come to me, and do not hinder them, for the kingdom of God belongs to such as these" (Luke 18:16).

By the time 1970 rolled around, things were going well for us. I'd been promoted to captain. The North Carolina property was paid off, and we had purchased a home in the same community where we'd been renting. I'd even bought a new 1970 Chevrolet pickup truck with the idea of some day using it on the farm. Our four girls were growing up, and Charlotte no longer complained about the property.

God's Word was impacting my life as I continued to feast on it daily. I had even started teaching a teenage Sunday School class —speaking aloud. But I was still too shy to pray aloud, so I would suggest we open class with silent prayer or would ask one of the teenagers to pray. But all in all, my relationship with God was growing stronger each day.

I knew in my heart that someday I'd be used by God to openly share about my relationship with Him. This feeling was dramatically confirmed by an unusual dream. It happened one afternoon, following a particularly tiring flight. I came home, changed out of my uniform, flopped into my favorite recliner, and switched on the TV. The family was in another part of the house doing their thing, and the TV program was boring, so I soon drifted off to sleep.

And soon, I began dreaming that I was sitting in a straight-back rocking chair—the only piece of furniture—in a large colonial-style room with high ceilings. The outside wall that I was facing contained two tall, narrow windows opened from the bottom. There were thin lace curtains adorning the windows, and they were blowing inward by a gentle, cool breeze. It was very relaxing.

I was startled by a small model airplane that came flying through the window to my left and was towing a white silk banner. On it in three-inch-high, black letters was the word *professionals*. The little airplane circled around my chair once and started to fly out the window to my right. *I must learn the meaning of this*, I thought to myself, so I reached up and grabbed the plane by its spinning propeller. When I did, a powerful electrical shock went down my arm and through my body. "My soul," I yelled, "it's of the Spirit." Immediately, I was jolted upright and awake.

The dream was so shocking and real that I knew it held some significant meaning. So I lay back in my recliner, closed my eyes, and began to pray. "God, this dream was too real not to have come from You. Please show me its meaning," I prayed. All at once, I was strangely aware of the television. I recognized the voice of Johnny Cash and opened my eyes to see him looking directly into the camera lens, telling what Jesus Christ had done for him. As I listened to Johnny's words, God began to speak to me—not in audible words but to my spirit.

He said, "I'm raising up professional people from all areas of life who will share the reality of Christ in their lives, and you will be one of those professionals."

There was no doubt in my heart that the dream would be fulfilled. I watched in the days to come as it began to happen and then gained momentum. The victors, the heroes of nearly every sporting event, began—more than ever before—giving credit for their success to God. Famous movie stars, entertainers, and musicians of all sorts started giving testimony of how Jesus was able to put their broken lives back together again. Doctors, lawyers, judges, politicians, military officers, and, yes, even airline pilots were doing the same. I was confident that some day I would be joining them. The dream helped solidify this confidence.

It didn't take long after the dream for God to reveal dramatically another portion of His plan for Charlotte and me. It happened one day while I was reading the eighteenth chapter of Luke's Gospel. Since I had started teaching Sunday School to teenagers, the plight of our nation's young people had been acutely brought home to me—broken homes, poverty, drugs, alcohol, unwholesome peer pressure, and even the removal of honoring God in our classrooms. So my heart was ripe for plucking that day as I read the words of Jesus and felt His compassion: "Let the little children come to me." Just those few words stirred a burning desire within me to do something in Jesus' behalf for children. "Lord," I cried, "How can I help? What can I do to bring the children to You?"

His answer was instantaneous: "You know that piece of property in North Carolina—the one that *I* provided? Well, it would make a beautiful place for the children to come to Me."

And for the first time it all made sense, the pieces began to fall in place. There had been nothing coincidental in my buying that property, in the marvelous way Charlotte had fallen in love with the out-of-doors, or in the way we both had been growing spiritually. God had been carrying us toward His plan the whole time. Why had I not seen from the beginning how perfectly suited our property was for constructing a camp: a Christian youth camp!

I knew by then that the acid test to the authenticity of this sudden inspiration would be Charlotte's reaction to it. If God was calling us into a Christian camp ministry, it would be as a team. I think the magic happened for Charlotte when I said the word *camp.* She was sold on the idea immediately. So talking, planning, and daydreaming about the camp became our prime topic of conversation. We didn't always see eye to eye on just how the plan was to be fulfilled, but there was never a doubt that God had called us to do it, and we were eager to meet the challenge given to us by God.

One of the drawbacks was that I still couldn't pray publicly. Charlotte kidded me a lot about my fear, saying, "How can we go down there and operate a Christian camp when you can't even pray in front of your own family—not even so much as at mealtime?"

"I don't know," I'd respond, "but I'm sure God has the answer. When the time is right, He'll take care of it."

In the meanwhile, I didn't have time to worry about it. There was too much preparation that had to be accomplished. It would take several more years before the children could come!

10
The Home the Lord Built

Unless the Lord builds the house,
its builders labor in vain (Ps. 127:1).

Before we could consider establishing a camp on our property, we first had to build a home. But we didn't want to move until I could be transferred to Atlanta, which was then a couple of years away. However, we were too excited merely to sit around. We borrowed a stack of magazines on house plans from friends and soon began poring over them. After months of doing this, we were still undecided. We wanted a house of modest size and inexpensive with a cathedral ceiling, a balcony, and a cozy fireplace. Nothing seemed to meet our expectations.

Finally, I decided to return the magazines, but when I picked them up, the top one fell out of my arms and landed open on the floor. When I stooped to pick it up, my eyes fastened on the picture of the most beautiful two-story, ranch house I had ever seen. One end of the house was ground level and the other underground. The house had a large rock chimney, using natural stone, but the most unusual feature about the house was the end partially underground. It was pointed and had a wraparound balcony angled out at the top—like the bow of a ship. And the house was surrounded by pines, exactly like the one we had selected for our dream house.

I was spellbound until I realized how big it was and how much it would cost to build and decided that was probably not for us. Yet, that special feeling stuck with us. When Charlotte came in, I pointed to the picture without uttering a sound. She quietly studied it for a moment. "That's it!" she squealed. "That's the house we're to build."

Charlotte's mom and dad, Mr. and Mrs. Andersen, were in the building and remodeling business and owned their own retail store specializing in floor covering, kitchens, and bathrooms. Mr. Andersen was thrilled with the plans. "O. A.," he said, "if you'll be your own general contractor, we can save you a lot of money."

"But I've never even built a doghouse, let alone a real house," I said.

"You can do it," he said, "and I'll help you. I'll even build your cupboards and vanities to specification here, haul them down, and install them for you. I can also save you money on materials by buying wholesale. How's that for a bargain?"

So with his encouragement, I went to North Carolina and legally established myself as a contractor, secured an estimated materials' cost, and swung a construction loan from the local bank.

The next person God led me to was Buren Walker, a retired building contractor. He was handy and lived less than a mile from our property. He came highly recommended by Uncle Frank. Even though Buren was retired as a contractor, he still knew everybody in the building trade and was respected by the community. We hit it off, so Buren insisted on working for us, just as a carpenter.

Still thinking we had plenty of time to complete the house, Buren and I began clearing out an acre lot from a forest of young pine trees. It was a gorgeous place situated at the foot of a small mountain—Cherry Mountain—that rose about 300 feet above us. The lot sloped gently up from a two-lane, black-topped road, and we looked across the road to rolling country-side which abruptly butted the Blue Ridge Mountains some forty miles to the west—a scene for some of the most spectacular sunsets God ever painted.

After the lot was cleared, I had Buren build a storage building to house our tools, supplies, water pump, and tank after our well was dug. Then he and I laid off the house site so the basement could be excavated.

Once the basement portion of the house was dug out, we were stuck with a hole in the ground through some harsh winter months until the masonry contractor, whom Buren had secured, could lay the foundation blocks. That was completed in the spring of 1972.

Carlos McGinnis, another reputable builder, contracted with me to put the house under roof and dried in. Buren worked with Carlos as part of his carpenter crew. In no time at all, they had the first floor framed out and were ready to lay the floor joist to begin the second floor.

Fortunately, God worked it out so I was available the day this was to begin. Buren was off. When I arrived at the site a few minutes after the workers, Carlos was standing at the edge of the yard looking down at two steel I-beams that had just been delivered—each forty feet long. He was rubbing his chin while his crew stood around aimlessly kicking the dirt. "What's wrong?" I asked, walking over to them.

"Just trying to figure out how we're going to get these beams in place," he said. "Each one of them must weigh a ton. It'll probably take fifteen men to set them." The house was eighty feet long, and the two beams bolted together were to be the center support for the floor joist.

"Know where we can get a crane?" I asked.

"Nope, but even if I did, it'd take a day or two to get it here, and then it'll cost you an arm and a leg." Then after some thought, he continued, "Your best bet's Reese and Sons over in Rutherfordton."

"Carlos," I said. "This is the Lord's house we're building. Maybe if we pray, He'll give us favor." He bowed his head with me as I silently asked God to help us. I still couldn't pray audibly in front of people. I did say "Amen" aloud, and then I asked Carlos, "Now, tell me how to get to Reese and Sons."

After hearing his instructions, I took off, leaving Carlos standing there scratching his head. Going to Rutherfordton required about twenty minutes. When I pulled into the drive at Reese and Sons, one of the sons was just stepping down from the cab of a mobile crane.

"What can I do for you?" he asked.

"I need that crane," I said.

"Man, is this your lucky day! I just got canceled off a job. Where's your place at?" he asked.

"Follow me, and I'll show you," I told him.

He laughed and said, "Lead on!"

I'll never forget the look on Carlos's face when in less than an hour I was back with a crane right behind me. He must have had some faith, however, because he and his men already had temporary posts in place ready to receive the beams. In less than thirty minutes, the beams were secured in place.

When Mr. Reese was finished, I asked, "How much do I owe you?" He was still laughing about the whole deal as he rewound his cable. "Well, you caught me at the right time and saved me a wasted half-day. How's twenty-five dollars sound?"

"Sounds good to me," I said. While pulling out my billfold, I couldn't help but glance over at the startled look on Carlos's face.

"You really believe in this prayer stuff, don't you?" he asked as the crane pulled away.

"Sure do, Carlos. With me, it's a way of life," I explained.

Then it was back to D.C. to fly my next trip. But in a few days, God had me back at the property in time to prevent another crisis. While I was away, the men had made good progress. The subflooring had been laid, and they had just finished putting down the wall templates and were getting ready to stud out the second floor. Carlos was beaming with pride, "O. A.," he said, "there's been a little mistake in measurement, but I've taken care of it."

"What kind of mistake?" I asked.

"Well, the house is six inches narrower than the plans call for," he said.

"How did that happen?" I asked.

"It's the twelve-inch block you used," he said. Then it dawned on me. The plan had called for a nine-inch poured basement wall. We had decided twelve-inch blocks would serve better. But we hadn't counted on the wall plates having to sit on the inside of the blocks, causing us to lose the six inches.

"How are you allowing for the difference?" I asked.

"Well, we can't make the hall any narrower," he said. "So we've taken three inches off the back rooms and three off the front."

That would have been super except Charlotte's dad was building our kitchen cupboards and bathroom vanities to the print specifications. If we used Carlos's idea, the vanities wouldn't fit into the bathrooms located on the back part of the house.

"Won't work," I said, explaining to him why.

"Boy!" he responded. "It's a good thing you showed up when you did, or we would have had a real problem on our hands." Then with a smile, he added. "Looks like the Lord is still looking over us."

Soon Carlos was nearing the completion of his contract. The outside of the house had been paneled where appropriate with plywood underlay and was ready for the rock masons. My first real problem arose when I couldn't find the two particular rock masons I wanted. This was one time even Buren, who seemed to know everything, couldn't help me. The masons had put a rock face on the Mooneyham Library in the nearby town of Forest City, and I loved it—the colorful natural stone they used and their craftsmanship. That was the stone and the craftsmanship I wanted for our house, and I was determined to find those two men.

However, several trips to North Carolina and wild goose chases throughout the region had turned up nothing—not even a trace.

One evening I was moping about the problem when Charlotte suggested, "Why don't you relax and forget about the house for a while? In fact, Why don't you go with me to PTA tonight? I'd like for you to meet Mrs. Queens, the new principal."

"Sure, why not? I don't get to attend PTA that often," I said.

Mrs. Queens had charm and a quick smile that put people at ease immediately. "Hear you fly for Eastern," she said when Charlotte introduced us.

"That's right," I said.

"Then maybe you know my nephew. He flies for Eastern, too. His name is Steve Thompson," Mrs. Queens said.

"Steve Thompson from Bat Cave, North Carolina?" I asked.

"Yes, that's right. Do you know him?" she asked.

"Sure do! In fact, I knew Steve even before I went to work for Eastern. Are you from North Carolina, too?" I wondered aloud.

"Certainly am, all my family's from the Bat Cave area," she explained. Bat Cave was a little mountain town near the summer resort area of Chimney Rock and Lake Lure—a place filled with beautiful rock work.

"Do you happen to know any rock masons?" I asked.

"Well, yes. As a matter of fact, two of my brothers, Paul and Woody Pryor, are rock masons. They're good ones too, I might add," Mrs. Queens told me.

My heart began to do flips. Could it be them? It'd be just like the Lord to do something like this—always making sure I knew who was really in control.

I told her about the two mystery masons whose work I'd so admired and how I had been trying to locate them: "It just might be Paul and Woody." She laughed as she dug in her purse for Paul's telephone number.

By the time I'd talked to Paul on the phone, I wasn't even surprised to find out that he and his brother were indeed the two I had been looking for. I made an appointment for Charlotte and me to visit him on an upcoming trip we had planned to North Carolina.

During that visit, we agreed on a contract for Paul and Woody to do our rock work, but the only drawback was we would have to wait on them until the spring of 1973. That didn't seem to be a problem at the time because we figured it would be longer than that before I could be transferred to Atlanta.

With that problem solved, things were really moving along smoothly. We were nearing the girls' summer break from school, and Charlotte had a full list of summer activities lined up for them, including a competitive meet in Buffalo for Cheryl and Lisa's majorette team, which Charlotte had agreed to host. This would leave me free during the summer to go and help Buren on the house on my days off. So at last, everything was under control.

Or I thought it was—until I learned that my transfer had been approved for me to be in Atlanta by October 1. And, suddenly, there was panic with Charlotte insisting that the girls should start the new school year in North Carolina, in late August.

By the time school was out, our lives were a flurry of activities. Charlotte took the girls to Buffalo for two weeks to fulfill her obligation to the majorette competition, while I spent a block of days off working on the house. Buren's grandson, Mike, was helping so we could get the house livable as soon as possible. Meanwhile, we turned our home in Virginia over to a realtor in hopes of a quick sale. I wanted $40,000 for the house, but the realtor talked me into lowering my price to $39,500 to help move it more quickly.

In order for me to stay in contact with Charlotte and Eastern when we first started the new house, I had a telephone installed in a wooden box mounted on a pole in the front yard. But when the house was closed in, and the phone was moved inside, it didn't work! I called the phone company, and they promised to have it fixed right away. But that day passed, and the next, and the next, and still it wasn't fixed. By then, I was ranting and raving. Buren merely looked at me and smiled. He knew this wasn't my normal character. But Mike, whom I had been trying to witness to about the Lord, thought my carrying on was funny.

When I went to have lunch with Aunt Eddy on the fourth day of the phone being out, there was a message for me to call my realtor in Virginia.

"O. A.!" he exclaimed. "Where have you been? I've been trying to call that treehouse phone of yours for four days. But let me tell you what's happening. You'd just left here when I got a buyer for your house. One look and he was ready to pay. But, now listen to this, another buyer has come along. He knows about the first buyer's offer, and he's willing to meet that plus paying your part of the closing cost. That'll net you $500 more. I guess it was good that I couldn't get you at first. Because now I can present you both offers."

There was nothing hard about that decision. I accepted the $500 more. The realtor said he would have the sale ready to sign when I came home. As soon as I got back to work after lunch, however, my conscience began bothering me. I apologized to Mike for the way I had been carrying on.

"Oh, that's OK," he said, "I would have been doing the same thing."

"No, I was wrong. My actions prove that I wasn't trusting God with the situation. But I'm sure glad He didn't listen to my complaining and let it get fixed." I chuckled.

"Why not?" Mike asked, puzzled.

"Because that phone being out of service made me $500," I told him.

Mike came flying down from his stepladder. "This I gotta hear," he said. And he just stood there shaking his head as I told him what had happened in the sale of the house. No sooner had I finished telling Mike the story than the telephone rang.

"Hello, is this Captain Fish?" came a cheerful lady's voice.

"Yes, it is," I answered.

"This is the operator," she said, "It appears your phone is working OK now?"

"Yes, praise the Lord, so it is," I said. Even amid the turmoil, the experience was like God had just called and said, "Hello, I'm still here."

When Charlotte finished in Buffalo, she and the girls came to North Carolina. We moved in our house and roughed it for a while. Charlotte cooked our meals on a hot plate and washed our dishes in the bathtub. Buren even had to tack plywood over our front entrance when he went home at night. When school started, the girls couldn't wait to come home every day to see what had been accomplished. Charlotte's mom and dad came down with the kitchen and bathroom fixtures and spent a few days while we all worked together to get them installed. Every day was like a picnic when we would spread our lunch out on the floor.

By the time fall had arrived, we still didn't have our heating system installed. Our contractor, it seemed, was having financial problems. Once again, we called on God for help. It wasn't fun taking baths on chilly mornings. Jack Harrison, another talented neighbor, came to our rescue. He not only improved the design of our heating system, he saved us hundreds of dollars on the installation—just before it turned cold.

By that winter, the house was almost completed except for the rock work. It wasn't pretty with tar paper tacked over the outside plywood, but we were comfortable. Paul and Woody Pryor were a welcomed sight when they showed up the next spring with a load of rocks, sand, and mortar ready to go to work. The rocks they brought were beautiful. Some were field stone, others had been bulldozed out of a mountain, and the rest they'd picked out of a mountain stream that flowed next to Paul's house. The colors in the rocks contained all the spectrums of white, blue, brown, black, gray, and in between.

The pair were more than rock masons, they were artists. Each stone they laid was as skillfully selected and placed as the brush stroke of a master artist. We all enjoyed watching them by the hour.

One day Woody noticed that Charlotte had stopped watching and was playing around with his rock pile, moving them around on the ground, arranging them first one way, then another.

"What are you trying to make?" he asked.

"A fish," she replied. "I'd like to have some rocks that form a fish right there," pointing to a spot on the front side of the house under the balcony.

"Well, you've got your wish." Woody said. "God formed stone just like that thousands of years ago, and I saw it yesterday up on the side of the mountain." He stood there a moment thinking about it. "That's a real nice idea—a fish to let people know that the Fishes live here!" he chuckled.

"No," Charlotte shook her head. "The fish would be to let people know that Christians live here." Charlotte had been studying early Christian symbols and knew the fish was a secret symbol which was used to identify themselves to each other without letting Roman persecutors know. The next day, a large sun fish appeared to be swimming across the rock on the front side of our house.

A few days later, they were rocking up the back wall of our fireplace which also happens to be the wall adjacent to the entrance steps of our front foyer. Due to the cathedral ceiling in the foyer, that particular wall was quite high. They were about halfway up with the rocks, when it dawned on me that we needed something to break the monotony of the flat rock wall.

When I mentioned this to Paul and Woody, they agreed. "What would you like?" Woody asked.

"How about a cross?" I asked.

"That would be nice," Woody said. He stopped and thought for a moment. "I remember seeing some long, flat rocks lying out back. See if you can find what you like, and we'll set them in."

I spotted a long, slender rectangular stone leaning against the rock pile, its base covered with heavy green and brown moss, ideal for the trunk of the cross. And with a little scratching around, I found another stone for the cross arm, and then another stubby rectangle-shaped stone with a jagged upper end just right for topping off the cross. I carried them around and placed them on the scaffolding with Paul and Woody. They looked at the wall, visually centering the cross from front to back and began to insert the rocks at the level where they were working—about halfway up. They installed the cross so that it protruded out about an inch from the face of the other rock.

However, the cross became most memorable to me one night some time later, when I turned into our driveway and noticed it glowing through a picture window. The light from the chandelier was reflecting off its protruded surface bathing it in a halo. A warm feeling engulfed me as I realized more than ever that God's love truly did build our home. He'd begun in our hearts and worked outward.

11

Harry Cherry and Isothermal Community College

Trust in the Lord with all your heart
and lean not on your own understanding;
in all your ways acknowledge him,
and he will make your paths straight (Prov. 3:5-6).

Once we had become settled in our new home, Charlotte and I were eager to get started developing what we thought would be a relatively simple project, turning some of our wooded area into a primitive campsite. It was fun batting ideas back and forth. Maybe we could clean out one of the springs to get drinking water, dig a pit for an outhouse, and put up some pup tents for sleeping. It sounded so simple and workable. But we were doing too much talking and not enough working. We needed a lightning bolt of some sort to get us started. Fortunately for us, however, God doesn't usually use lightning bolts. Sometimes, He sends a visitor, like He did with us.

We were sitting at the kitchen table one morning discussing our dream camp when an unexpected visitor arrived. The permanent steps from our basement floor to the second floor had still not been completed. We were talking when we heard someone climbing up the temporary ladder outside the basement which lead to the foyer landing. We could see the back of his head as he came up, moving slowly and cautiously, and we stopped talking until he reached the landing and turned around.

It was Harry Cherry, the local soil conservation agent. I had met with him on several occasions to discuss and develop a land management program for the property. "Hello, Harry," I said.

Startled, he began to sputter, "I, I'm sorry. I didn't know anybody was home. What I mean is I didn't even know you had moved in."

"It's OK," we said, laughing. "Other people have made the same mistake. The house certainly doesn't look livable." We invited him to have a cup of coffee, and after exchanging greetings, he reached into his briefcase and pulled out some forms. "I'm really glad to catch you, O. A. We need to get started developing a farm plan for that last sixty-seven acres you bought."

Charlotte and I had recently purchased the land from our neighbor, Virgil Womack. It extended our boundary to the top of Cherry Mountain, and it was ideal for our proposed camp.

"That's great, Harry. In fact, I was planning on coming in to see you. I certainly want to manage the land that God has intrusted to us well. But Harry, our real plans are to develop a Christian youth camp." He sat up, and an astounded expression crossed his face.

"What's this about a camp?" Harry asked.

"We want to build a Christian camp," I repeated.

"Well, then maybe you two might like to take a course on outdoor development and recreation?" Harry asked.

"I don't know. Where is the course, and what's it all about?" I asked, curiously.

"It'll be at ICC, Isothermal Community College, and, basically, it'll be a course on how to build a camp. We already have the curriculum established and the instructors lined up, the whole bit. And all we need are two more people to have the minimum required for funding." Harry explained.

Now it was our turn to be startled. *This has to have come from God,* I thought. Harry even had application forms with him which we filled out, and two weeks later the course began. It met for three hours every Thursday evening and continued for ten weeks. The long list of experts who taught, lectured, and shared testimonies covered every phase imaginable, concerning building and managing a camp which included all the legal, health, and safety regulations. They talked about organizational planning, developing planning, soil conservation, horticulture, wildlife, nature trails, lake construction and management, waterfront safety, health department requirements concerning food preparation and serving, drinking water, and sewer systems. They talked about the various successes and pitfalls experienced by other camps operating in our area.

Perhaps even more miraculous was the fact that I didn't miss a single moment of any class—even though I was commuting to Atlanta and flying reserve. Reserve flying meant I only had ten scheduled days off each month and was subject to be called out the rest of the time—twenty-four hours a day. So I was also required to be at the airport and in uniform ready to go within two and a half hours of any quick call out. And my electing to live two hundred and eleven miles from the airport was not an acceptable excuse for delaying a flight. But, not only did I make every class at ICC, I never missed or delayed a flight while the class was going on. I discovered during those ten weeks that God was also a master crew scheduler.

When the course was completed, Charlotte and I brought home enough resource material to fill a library. We should have been experts on camp building by then, but the effect was just the opposite. So much information had been thrown at us in such a short period that it was like trying to get a drink of water from a fire hydrant. Most of it passed us by. The one thing we did learn for sure was there was no such thing as building a simple primitive-type camp like we'd envisioned. The complexity of camp building had so overwhelmed us that we were ready to give up the whole idea.

One night after looking over all the resource information and my notes from the class again, I felt like I just had to get out of the house and be alone with God. In the dark, I made my way down to our pasture and sat down on an old power pole that had been left lying there on the grass. I was ready to resign. "God," I said, "You know how much I wanted to build a camp for You, but they won't allow me to build a simple camp like I'd know how to do, and I'm not qualified to build what they require. I don't have the expertise or the money or the time. So, I just wanted to tell You, even though I still want to do it, I just can't. I guess You'll have to find someone who's more qualified than me to build Your camp."

After saying my piece, I was ready to leave, but God wasn't finished with me. Within my heart He began speaking to me clearer than I'd ever heard before— not in an audible voice, but nonetheless His words came pouring through my mind: "I didn't call you to build a camp for hurting children because you were qualified," He said, "but because you were willing. I have the know-how. If you'll just give Me one day at a time, commit the beginning of each day to Me and watch, and together we'll build a camp. And I'll raise up experts to assist you in every area where you have a need." For a long time I couldn't get up from that old pole. I was in a holy place, and my heart was filled with worship and praise.

When I was finally able to arise, there was a new get-up-and-go in my spirit. Charlotte could tell without a word when I got back that I had a new sense of confidence and peace within myself. But the experience had been so personally moving that it took me couple of days before I was able to tell her about it.

It would have been nice if everything had fallen into place after that night, and our camp had gone into operation soon thereafter, but it didn't happen that way. He still had a lot of preparation to complete in me first.

But what did happen was that I began awakening early every morning, and the first words that came to mind were: "Good morning, Lord. What's in store for today?" Then I would get up while it was still quiet and spend time alone with God, reading His Word. Slowly I began to relax and then eventually to trust and acknowledge His guidance more and more. But, the more I trusted, the more I found that His directions were sometimes anything but relaxing.

12
The Hopewell Hoodlums

I am going to send you what my Father has promised; but stay in the city until you have been clothed with power from on high (Luke 24:49).

Even after my unique experience with the Lord sitting on the old power pole in the pasture, I was still hindered by a phobia about sharing Him with others. I still could not pray aloud— even with my own family. Yet, I knew that this was another area in my life that God was going to fix, if I was going to be able to operate a Christian camp. And another thing that was about to be fixed, which I wasn't aware of, was my vision for the camp ministry. I had envisioned sitting around a camp in a primitive setting and teaching the Bible to a small group of well-mannered, well-groomed, typical Sunday-School-type kids. I could just see them sitting there at my feet with their mouths open, like hungry little birds, waiting for me to feed them the Word of God.

But it sure didn't take God long to show me differently. I came home from a flight one afternoon to find about a dozen hippie-type boys sitting on our front stoop talking to Barbara and Cheryl, our two young teenage daughters. I angrily pushed my way through them to get to the front door. "What's with him?" I heard one of them ask as I went inside and bounded up the steps in our foyer looking for Charlotte.

When I found her standing at the sink, nonchalantly washing dishes, my anger was quickly directed toward her. *How dare she permit that gang of low-lifes to associate with our daughters,* I thought. Steam must have been pouring from my nostrils. Grabbing her by the left shoulder, I spun her around. "Who is that gang down there talking to Barbara and Cheryl?" I demanded.

She pulled loose from my grip and turned back toward the sink. Then she said softly, "I don't know. I guess they're your first group of kids to work with."

Her words pounded my brain like a jackhammer. I was stunned. It took several moments to gather my composure, but I knew what I had to do. I swallowed hard and practically crawled back down the steps to where the young people were gathered.

"Hi, guys," I said sheepishly.

"Hi," a couple of them chorused as they all glared at me in disbelief. "Who are you guys?"

"The Hopewell Hoodlums," one of them remarked. They all giggled. Hopewell was a nearby community.

"You guys messing with drugs?" was my next question. "Yeah," two or three of them confessed as they looked at each other shrugging their shoulders. The one who appeared to be the most boisterous of them said, "We smoke a little pot and drink some beer."

"How about the law? Any of you in trouble with the law?" I asked.

"Sure," they again confessed. They were totally disarming me with their honesty. A couple said they had been arrested for knocking down rural mailboxes, but they admitted they were all guilty. The rest of them had outrun the law. Before I knew it, we were all relaxing, laughing, talking, and becoming friends. As I listened to their stories, they stole my heart. Each came from a totally different background, but they all had one thing in common. None of them had a normal father-son relationship. One had no idea who his father was. One had recently learned his last name when he'd secured his birth certificate to get his driver's license. The others had fathers, but they were all estranged because of serious problems—alcoholism, illness, illiteracy, and emotional instability. I was sure the boys packed together for mutual support, and I knew with no moral standards or guidance, they were headed for trouble. Neither Charlotte nor I had had any training in psychology. And I couldn't even minister to them about my Christian faith, but God gave me a special love for those boys in the coming days. After setting down some guidelines, we began to let them come visit Friday nights and weekends. We couldn't make them go to school, but we let them know that we'd be no part of their excuses for not going. We set an 11:00 p.m. curfew for their leaving when they did come. And once again, we told them we knew we couldn't make them go home, but we would not be used as an excuse for their not going. When I discovered there was a youth revival going on in the area, I became excited.

These meetings had started out as a week-long revival at one of the local Methodist churches with kids from every denomination attending. And at the end of the week, the youth hadn't wanted it to stop, so they had decided to meet one Sunday evening every month at a different church. *Maybe if I can get our boys to attend these revivals, they'll be saved,* I thought, *and I'll be let off the hook and won't have to share Christ with them myself.*

The boys were glad to go. They were always ready to go with us anywhere. But the clothes they wore were not exactly suitable, and there was always a problem getting them to the church on time. Every time we went, the church was filled to capacity, and we were late. The services would come to a complete halt while I came in with the bunch of ragtags, looked around for a seat, and ended up sitting on the floor of the aisles or disrupting the services while someone dragged out extra chairs. But the revival services were great. Dozens of youth were turned on for the Lord, yet to my disappointment, none of our guys seemed all that touched.

The only time I saw them emotional was when someone was extra kind to them. The first Christmas after we'd met them, Charlotte made them each a stocking with their names embossed and filled them with fruits, nuts, candy, and gifts. And when the boys arrived that Christmas morning and saw the stockings stretched across the mantle of our rock fireplace, every one of them had tears in his eyes. It was the first time I'd seen any of them cry.

As time went on, we became closer and closer to the guys. When they were with us, they were well behaved and polite. They had even improved somewhat in the way they dressed, but

Charlotte and I suspected that when they were on their own, they were their old devilish selves. We also suspected that the culprit who was causing this behavior was Billy Ayers. Billy was nineteen, much older than most of the guys. He was deemed unteachable and incorrigible; he had been kicked out of school when he was in the sixth grade at the age of sixteen. When he was with us, Billy was always polite, but he had small, beady eyes that glared from beneath long stringy hair, and his conversation seldom went beyond, "Yes Ma'am, No Ma'am, Yes Sir, No Sir."

We knew once the boys were away from us, Billy was leading them to make trouble. We were told that he was drinking, smoking pot, and living with an older woman. We felt Billy was beyond hope, that even God couldn't help him. So Charlotte and I began devising a plan whereby we could drive a wedge between Billy and the boys, hoping we could get them away from his bad influence. When the time was right, we planned to stop him from coming to the house altogether.

But in the meantime, I had learned that Campus Crusade for Christ had begun a new high school ministry, and I thought it would be great if I could interest them in coming into our local high schools. I wrote to the ministry's outreach center in Atlanta, and a few weeks later I received a telephone call in response. They were willing to send George Tucker, one of their high school directors, to spend a couple of days with me, if I would make arrangements for him with some of the local church youth groups. Of course, I was glad to do this, so the date was set for George's coming.

Charlotte and I both fell in love with George the minute he showed up at our house. He was young, good-looking, and an ex-football player with a beautiful spirit. He also struck it off with our boys right away. Several churches had agreed for him to speak to their youth over the weekend, but I had purposely kept Saturday evening free for him to spend with our boys. We had built a horse ring in our pasture that was equipped with lights, so George and the boys decided to go down there and play touch football.

I noticed that Billy had taken a real liking to George. He never seemed to leave George's side. In the past, Billy had always

shied away from strangers. However, after the football game was
over and while everyone was still laughing, slapping each other
on the back, and bragging about the great plays they'd made,
George and Billy walked off down into the pasture by themselves. In a little while, they came back and strolled over to
where I was standing. I noticed Billy had been crying.

"O. A.," George said, "Billy has something he wants to tell
you."

"What is it?" I asked.

Billy stood there, looking down at the ground, with his hands
thrust into his pockets. Almost shyly, he said, "Mr. Fish, I just
asked Jesus to come into my heart." Then he looked up with a
smile. I had never seen Billy smile like that before. God, using
George Tucker, had brought the impossible. Oh, how I longed
to be used by God like that.

We found as the days passed that Billy's conversion was no
con game. The day after George left, Billy came to Charlotte and
asked her to cut about an inch off his stringy hair. A few days
later, another inch came off. And a few days later, another inch.
Soon he was going to a hair stylist. After a while, people didn't
recognize him, but it wasn't because of the change in his physical
appearance as much as the beautiful change that had taken place
in his personality. Even with his limited ability, Billy began reading the New Testament that George had given him. He'd struggle each day to read one page, and then come to me to see if he
understood what he'd read. His simple childlike faith and his
tremendous spiritual insight concerning the Scriptures astounded me.

During this time, my own chronic phobia had reached a point
of desperation. I felt that if God didn't do something soon to
help me tell others about Him like George had done for Billy, I
would die. And as it always seemed to be with me, it was at this
point of desperation that God once again took control. He
showed me that I had harbored a critical condemning spirit toward the belief of others, and this had to change before He
could use me as I asked.

An incident that had occurred just before we left Alexandria,
Virginia, came back to me. Tom and Lydia Crim, an Assembly of

God couple, had moved in from Oklahoma and started attending our church: Faith United Methodist. I'd told myself to stay away from these suspected "Holy Rollers," but somehow they'd talked Charlotte into attending special Monday night services and weekday Bible studies. She would come home from these meetings, excited, trying to tell me about the praise and worship, and talking about the miracles she'd witnessed. But I always stopped her by changing the subject. Finally, she stopped talking about the meeting altogether. *If she was happy, and that made her feel close to the Lord,* I thought, *that's fine with me.* I remembered how as a child we'd made fun of the Pentecostals, and I wanted no part of someone making fun of me. However, after a while, I did start attending some of the Bible studies. To my surprise, I enjoyed their Bible studies. All of us, whatever the denomination, are indwelt by the Holy Spirit, and we should fervently pray for the Holy Spirit to fill us—and keep us filled. Baptists, Methodists, Pentecostals, charismatics, you name 'em, desperately need the fire of the Holy Spirit. Every born-again believer is one in the Spirit with all his or her brothers and sisters in Christ.

Tom Crim had shaken my defense when I was giving him my talk about the gifts of the Spirit being for the illiterate and weaklings. "Do you think the apostle Paul was illiterate and weak?" he asked. And that was the end of the conversation. I had no comeback. I was strongly influenced by Pat Robertson's book: *Shout It from the Housetops.* He was an educated lawyer, an ordained Baptist minister, host of the "700 Club," and founder of the Christian Broadcasting Network.

Also, about the same time that we moved to North Carolina, WGGS-TV, a Christian television station out of Greenville, South Carolina, went on the air. Our reception wasn't good, so all we could receive was a fuzzy picture, but the sound came in well. This station carried the "700 Club," and after having read Pat's book, I watched it faithfully.

Not long after, I was in a hotel room in Atlanta—again watching the "700 Club." The program being aired that night had nothing to do with the fruits and gifts of the Spirit, yet I had a tremendous conviction to kneel by the bedside and ask

God's forgiveness for the judgmental attitude I had been harboring against some of His people. A warm feeling engulfed me as I prayed: "Lord, forgive me for judging, and, Lord, I realize the Holy Spirit lacks freedom to move in my own life, and I don't want it to be that way anymore. I want . . . I need all the help you have to offer me."

I didn't literally see Jesus that night, but the presence that filled the room was unmistakably His. I had never before experienced the worshipful spirit which came welling up from my innermost parts. The "sweet, sweet spirit" of the Holy Spirit engulfed me with warmth and overpowering love. I don't know how long this glorious experience lasted. It must have been forty-five minutes or longer, but when I got up off my knees, I was a changed person.

No sooner had I gotten home from that trip than all my girls began saying, "Something must have happened to Daddy." All I was able to do for days was go around crying unashamedly and talking about Jesus. I even said impromptu prayers at mealtime.

With this newfound boldness in my life, Charlotte and I decided to attend a Campus Crusade for Christ Lay Institute for Evangelism where we could learn to lead others to Christ like George Tucker had led Billy Ayers.

The first day home from the lay institute, I led Jay Brooks, a brother of one of the original Hopewell Hoodlums, in the sinner's prayer. And Charlotte, while sharing one of Campus Crusade's special booklets for children with our youngest daughter Kim, had the very special privilege of praying with her to ask Jesus to come into her heart.

Another result of the newfound power in my life and the training I had received was demonstrated one day in Atlanta. I went out on Peachtree Street and began sharing Christ with strangers. I had the opportunity to pray with four teenage boys to receive Christ, and I shared with an old, black gentleman who was pushing a laundry cart down the street. He didn't want to pray with me right then. However, as he was pushing his cart away, I could see tears streaming down his cheeks, and he was saying over and over, "I sure knows I need Jesus in my life.

After this, Charlotte and I were both so excited about what the lay institute had done for us that we decided that we wanted the boys and our daughters, Barbara and Cheryl, to experience the same training.

George Tucker had supplied us with information about an upcoming Campus Crusade for Christ high school Christmas conference to be held at Rock Eagle 4-H Camp in Eatonton, Georgia, during the Christmas to New Year's school break.

Barbara; Cheryl; their girl friend Janice Melton, who had also become one of "our kids"; and several of the boys were excited about going. We started planning in the fall, so that gave them about three months to raise the funds for the trip. They cut pulp wood, sold items, did housework and yard work, and anything else they could think of to make money. Due to my flight schedule and other commitments, neither Charlotte nor I could go, but Bruce and Doris Hamrick, the youth leaders from Salem United Methodist Church agreed to go in our place. Our family and most of the boys were members at that church. The youth finally earned enough money to pay their expenses with some extra to buy tracts and other evangelistic material for use when they came back.

We sent them off excited, the day after Christmas '73, and the tragic accident that took Barbara's life occurred on their way back home from the conference. But in spite of the tragedy, that week worked wonders in the lives of those young people. Many of them were instrumental in winning others to the Lord. Billy Ayers was sitting in the front seat with Barbara and Doris Hamrick when the accident happened. He told us that just before the accident they had been singing the Scripture songs they had learned at the conference, then seconds before impact, Barbara had said, "I can't wait to see Jesus."

After recovering emotionally from Barbara's death, Billy attended Isothermal Community College's Adult Education Lab and earned his high school diploma—another sign of the power of God in one's life. He later married Becky Biggerstaff, a girl he had helped nurture in the Lord, and the two of them adopted two beautiful daughters. Billy also became a youth leader at a Baptist church.

Watching God work in Billy's life has been one of my greatest pleasures. Never have I seen anyone whose spirit was as hungry as his. He didn't have to tarry as long as I did to experience Pentecost in his Christian walk. However, I had the pleasure of leading him there. I thank God for touching me with His power to be a witness, and I thank Him for the Hopewell Hoodlums who gave us our on-the-job training.

Part 2:
Fruitfulness in Ministry

Faith by itself, if it is not accompanied by action, is dead.
But someone will say, "You have faith; I have deeds."
Show me your faith without deeds, and I will show you my faith by what I do (Jas. 2:17-18).

The apostle Peter is often chided for a lack of faith because he took his eyes off Jesus and looked at the storm when he was attempting to walk on the water at Jesus' beckoning. But I feel confident that Peter always remembered those few steps he did take. He had the courage to get out of the boat. That, in some way, is how Charlotte and I feel about our experience at the camp. We may not have had perfect faith, but we've known the thrill of leaving the security of the boat and taking those first few steps.

Part 2 of *Fingerprints of God* tells some of the unique stories we have witnessed in seeing South Mountain Christian Camp brought into being a reality and through our moving toward the outstretched hand of Jesus. As our faith was put into action, so grew the camp; as the camp grew, so grew our faith.

13
Divine Appointees

Now faith is the substance of things hoped for, the evidence of things not seen. For by it the elders obtained a good report. Through faith we understand that the worlds were framed by the word of God, so that things which are seen were not made of things which do appear (Heb. 11:1-3, KJV).

Surely, South Mountain Christian Camp was framed by the Word of God that night while I sat on that old power pole out in our pasture. "If you give your life anew to Me each morning," He'd told me, "I'll raise up the needed expertise, and together we'll build the camp."

Leon Harkins was our first divine appointee. Leon had been one of our instructors at the Outdoor Recreation and Development course we took at ICC. He was introduced to us as the state's foremost expert on camp planning and developing, and when someone in the class asked him what chance one of us might have of acquiring his services, he answered, "None!" He then elaborated about his busy schedule. The thought crossed my mind, *That is, unless God decides otherwise.*

Not long after we'd completed the course, I called home from a hotel while on a layover. I was curious about how Charlotte's day had gone at a sports equipment seminar she had attended. We were hoping to impress some company into donating needed equipment.

"Boy, am I glad you called," she said, "Do I have some good news!"

"Somebody donated some equipment?" I guessed.

"Nope, nothing like that," she teased.

"Someone offered us a big discount on equipment then?" I guessed again.

"Nope. Wrong again." It was obvious she was getting a kick out of keeping me going with the guessing game.

Finally I said, "I give up. What's the good news?"

"We have someone who's going to develop the camp layout," she replied, unable to hide a little giggle.

My heart came up into my throat. Surely I had misunderstood her. "What do you mean—someone to develop the camp layout?"

"You know, you've been afraid that we couldn't afford a developer," she continued. This was true. In fact, I would have to handle that task by myself.

"And just how much is this person going to charge?" I stammered nervously.

"He's not going to charge anything!"

"Now wait a minute. Who is this guy?" I said. Surely this must have been a joke.

"Who would you like for it to be?" she asked, giggling again.

"Well," I answered. "It doesn't cost to wish. So why not Leon Harkins? They say he's the best."

"Then, your wish is granted. That's who it's going to be!" she exclaimed.

While I tried to regain my composure, Charlotte told me how she had met Leon at the seminar. "I was telling an archery supply salesman about our camp for disadvantaged youth when Leon walked up and began eavesdropping. Then Leon broke in and asked, 'Ma'am, don't I know you?' I told him we were in his class at ICC, and he answered, 'That's right. I remember you and your husband. I wondered why you two were there.' As we kept talking, he asked me who our development planner was.

"Nobody! We can't afford to hire one. And he said, 'I'll do it, and it won't cost you anything.'"

As she talked, I paced the room from side to side. Then I yelled aloud, unable to contain my excitement. I kept shouting, "Praise God! Thank you, Jesus! Hallelujah!"

As soon as I reached home from my flight I sent Leon a topographical map containing elevation contour lines of the area.

Soon thereafter he made an appointment to make an on-site survey. It was difficult for me to realize he was doing all of this for us, and he expected nothing in return.

When he arrived, we started walking throughout the property. It was amazing how well he already knew the layout of the land. He had practically memorized the map I'd sent him. As we went through forest and heavy undergrowth, I'd point out the remains of some old logging trail and comment, "Leon, I think it'd be pretty easy if we could make a road," or I'd suggest, "Leon, don't you think we should try to renovate that old barn?" But he would put his finger to his lips and go "Shhh" to shush me. And after little more than an hour, he flashed a satisfied smile, nodded, and we returned to the house.

A couple of months later, his drawings came in the mail. Charlotte and I were ecstatic over the layout—natural and logical. This experience made me aware of what a botched-up mess I'd have made of the layout if God had left the planning up to me.

Leon had strategically located the entrance road close to the area zoned for recreation—ball field, tennis courts, gym site, picnic area, and so forth. This overlooked an exquisite nine-acre lake site with cabins planned for either side. Then there was a multipurpose building that would contain office space, cafeteria, and an auditorium; there were trails, camp-fire circles, and much more. Charlotte and I both became excited as we examined every line on the drawings. My adrenaline was flowing, until Charlotte snapped me back into reality. "How in the world can we afford it?" she asked.

"By faith," I said trying to sound assuring. Then we thanked God for sending Leon to us to make our vision visible on paper. Now we could better communicate the vision to others—helping them see beyond the present wilderness maze of trees and heavy undergrowth to the finished product.

Finally, we had a plan for the camp's physical structure, but we still needed a non-profit legal structure. Charters and by-laws were Greek (or Sanscrit) to me. Obviously we needed a good lawyer, but who?

B. T. Jones, prominent lawyer and former member of the North Carolina state legislature, was highly respected in our county. As I was praying about needing a lawyer, God called B. T. Jones's name to mind. I knew B. T. only by reputation, but I remembered how Dee had always bragged on him. B. T. had been Dee's long-time Sunday School teacher. Dee used to declare that when he died he wanted B. T. to preach his funeral. "There is not another man in the world who knows his Bible better and is more respected," Dee stated.

Indeed, when Dee died, B. T. spoke at his funeral. As I listened to B. T.'s eulogy, I was even more impressed with B. T.'s spiritual qualities. I prayed, "Lord, are You saying I should ask B. T. Jones for his help?"

I was almost sure I heard God speaking to my heart, "I gave you Leon Harkins as a planner. Why not B. T. Jones as a lawyer?"

It was a few days before I had the courage to act on those words and approach B. T. Finally, with Leon's plans I visited B. T. He reminisced about his friendship with my dad. Then, acting as though he had just noticed the plans, he asked, "What do you have there?"

"Oh, oh," I stammered. "This is what I came to talk to you about." I unrolled the plans, spread them on B. T.'s desk, and began chattering about my dream camp.

As I rambled on, he leaned back in his swivel chair and put his hands behind his head. Then after a while, he stopped me. "We'll be glad to help," he said. Then he called his two secretaries, Doris and Sandra, into his office and introduced them to me. He briefly explained my vision for the camp and announced that he had volunteered their services toward helping me. They just stood there smiling and nodding their heads. By now I was choking back tears, grateful for God's faithfulness and these people who were so willing to help to make a dream come true.

They spent hours of time pouring over corporate law books, determined not to leave an *i* undotted or a *t* uncrossed in getting the camp properly and legally organized. Finally, the laborious task was completed. A charter, a set of bylaws, and a land-lease agreement had been forged, tailor-made to meet our needs. We submitted the whole package to North Carolina State and the Internal Revenue Service for approval to operate according to their respective codes as a nonprofit corporation. Within days we received our approval from North Carolina, but the situation was different with the Internal Revenue Service. Months of changes and resubmissions went by without final approval until I was about ready to again throw in the towel and give up. But I kept thinking, surely God hasn't brought us this far to let us down.

Joe Smart, an old general, aviation buddy of mine, was my next divine appointee. He held the key to God's answer. To worsen my woes concerning the IRS problem, I had been temporarily bumped out of Atlanta and back to Washington as a crew base. I spent a good deal of my off-duty time in D.C. with my brother, Eugene, who was a local used-car buyer.

We were sitting around at a car dealership in Springfield, Virginia, swapping stories when Joe's name came up. He ran a TV repair shop nearby. Joe was divorced, losing his wife and daughter by his drinking, and, eventually, his dad bought him a one-way bus ticket out-of-town. Joe's dad had told him that unless he gave up alcohol, he didn't want to see him again. Later, one Christmas morning, Joe awoke from a drunken stupor to find himself in a ditch along Route 1 just south of Alexandria, Virginia, and God in His mercy sent a member of Alcoholics Anonymous (AA) to rescue him. The man took Joe under his care, sobered him up, dried him out, and involved him in AA. That Christmas marked Joe's last drink. Joe had proudly invited me to his twelfth-year sobriety party at an AA meeting. By this time, he was remarried and operating a successful business.

After talking for a while, Eugene and I decided to pay Joe a visit. We were totally surprised by his greeting. "O. A.! Boy, am I glad to see you." He ran over and gave me a big hug. "I need a favor," he said.

"What kind of favor?" I asked.

"I'm worried sick about my dad. I haven't been able to get him on the phone for several days. His hearing is so bad that I don't know if there's something wrong or if he just isn't hearing the phone.

This is turning out to be a strange coincidence, I thought. Joe's dad and mom, before her recent death, lived not too far from me.

Now his dad was living alone. The evening before this visit I had been driving by the house and saw Mr. Smart sitting in the front yard. Knowing that he was probably lonely since his wife's death, I'd stopped, and we'd had a long chat together. He told me how proud he was of Joe.

"Your dad's doing great, Joe." I said. Then I told him about my visit the day before and how proud his dad was of him.

"God had to have sent you by this morning," Joe said, "because I've been praying for some word from Dad all morning. I've really been worried about him since Mom died with him there by himself."

"I'm sure you have, Joe, but he's doing fine. And tell you what, I'll keep a check on him for you, if you'd like? He lives so close that it is no problem." I told him.

"Oh, that would really be an answer to prayer," Joe responded.

"I've got something I would also like for you to pray about." I said.

"What's that?" Joe asked. Then I told him about how North Carolina approved our camp but that we were having problems getting approved by the IRS.

"That's strange," Joe said. "My wife just started a home for alcoholic women in North Carolina, and they're having just the opposite problem. They got IRS approval right away, but are having trouble with the state."

"How did you get approval from the IRS so fast?" I asked him.

He winked and said, "Because my best old, AA buddy is the head man over the nonprofit division of IRS. His office is in the Federal Building in Washington." By then my head was spinning. I knew that God was up to something again.

"Would there be any chance you might introduce me to this 'old friend'?" I asked.

"Sure," he said. "I'll be glad to."

Within two weeks, Joe had arranged the meeting. His friend John was every bit as nice as Joe described. It turned out that he was an old navy pilot, and the three of us spent an hour hangar flying. Finally, John said, "O. A., what's this Joe tells me about

the Christian Youth Camp you're building? I understand my
people are giving you a hard time."

Talking about flying had been fun and easy, but the minute I
started trying to talk about the camp, I became tongue-tied and
flustered. But John took the paperwork I had brought with me
and began reading. He was a speed-reader, and within minutes
he had read all the documents. Then he pointed out one by-law
that didn't comply with the IRS's requirement. He even told me
how to word the needed change.

"After you get this changed, resubmit the paperwork to the
Atlanta office, and if they kick it back again, then appeal it to
Washington," he paused, laughing, and went on, "That's me. So
don't worry. You've got your approval. Just keep up the good
work at the camp, and God bless you."

My feelings at that moment must have been like what Moses
felt when God saved him from Pharaoh by rolling back the Red
Sea, except in my case it was a sea of paperwork. It seemed that
the pharaohs of this world were still subject to the realm of God.
Within a few weeks after resubmitting, we were a federal and
state tax-exempt corporation.

During the formative years of South Mountain Christian
Camp, God brought many wonderful people to our aid, and
He's still bringing them—people who lend their expertise, their
muscle, and their talent. For instance, there is Sue Hardin, who
for years has given time to keeping our books and serving on our
board; Alfred Williamson, who prepared our tax returns; Linda
and Wayne Goode, who helped get the camp computer orientat-
ed; Bill Stallings, our health inspector; Harry Cherry and his
sidekick Jimmy Andrews, our soil conservation agents; Ed Bid-
dix, agriculture extension agent; Gilmer Edwards, Agriculture
Stabilization Conservation Services; Tim Gordon, engineer for a
local power company; plus numerous carpenters, electricians,
plumbers, and just plain handymen who provided immeasurable
help; and the vendors where we obtain building materials, food,
office supplies, and sporting equipment. There is no doubt that
God raised up all these people so that our every need has been
and is continuing to be met—just as He promised me that night

when I sat on that old power pole, discouraged, and ready to quit.

I've gotten to the place where every time I meet someone new to help with a need, I remember Hebrews 13:1-2: "Keep on loving each other as brothers. Do not forget to entertain strangers, for by so doing some people have entertained angels without knowing it."

14
Billy Ayers and the Trailer-Hitch Knob

I woke up this morning
And rushed into the day.
I had so much to accomplish,
I didn't take time to pray.
Troubles tumbled all about me,
Harder became each task.
Why doesn't God help me? I wondered,
And remembered, I hadn't asked.

But I got up this morning,
And prayed before entering the day.
I had so much to accomplish;
I had to take time to pray.
                    —Author Unknown

After the kids returned from the Campus Crusade Christmas Conference, Billy Ayers asked me if I could use him at our camp. There was a lot of work to be done, particularly clearing of the trees and heavy undergrowth. And I knew that by selling the trees for pulpwood, I could help underwrite Billy's salary, so I put him to work. Besides it would give me more time to share the Bible and enjoy Christian fellowship with him.

I instructed Billy in the beginning that when I was home from a flight, he was to meet me at my house by seven o'clock in the morning so we could have prayer together, plan the day, and be at work by eight. This worked well at first, but, gradually, he started showing up later and later. One day, he didn't show up until almost eight o'clock. I was so angry by the time he got there that I met him at the door with an angry: "Come on, Billy. We've got to get to work!"

He looked at me rather strange, as if to say: You mean we're not going to pray? But pretending I hadn't noticed, I said, "Come on. It's already getting hot, and we've got work to do." It was in the middle of July, and the days warmed up fast. There was nothing I disliked more than working through the heat of the day.

We were working along the streams where our lake site was to be, using our farm tractor with an old, metal, World War II jeep trailer behind it. The terrain was too rough for anything else to get in there. Billy backed the trailer up to where I had a big log waiting to throw on it. And when I did, the trailer hitch came loose from the tractor, and the trailer reared up with the tailgate almost hitting my foot.

After checking out the cause of the problem, we discovered that the threads on the ball joint shaft had stripped. This meant that I would have to run into town and buy a new one. That would cost another hour. When I got back from town with the new joint, Billy still hadn't gotten the old joint loose from the trailer tongue. That added to my frustration: *Why couldn't he accomplish a simple task like loosening the knob and slipping the ball joint out!*

"It won't come out, Mr. Fish," he said. "I've tried and tried."

"Here, let me try," I said pushing him back out of my way. "Hmmm," I said after discovering that he had indeed loosened the knob on the tongue all the way: "Why won't it come out?" No amount of prying, twisting, or tugging would get the ball joint to come out. By this time, the sun was high in the sky, and sweat was pouring off my reddened face.

Billy had gotten down on his knees in a kneeling position right under the trailer tongue and was patiently watching me. And after a while he said, "You know what, Mr. Fish?"

"No, Billy. What?" I snapped.

"We didn't pray this morning," he said.

If you had been there on time, we would have had time to pray, I thought to myself, but I didn't say anything. I just kept hopelessly twisting and tugging on the stuck ball joint.

"Well, Mr. Fish, what do you think we should do about it?" Billy inquired.

"Do about what!" I again snapped.

"Praying," he said.

And when I looked down into his pleading brown eyes, I was tremendously convicted. Without saying anything, I knelt down on one knee and laid my left hand on the trailer-hitch knob. And the moment my hand touched the knob, the ball joint fell out. Billy was looking directly at it when it fell. In fact, he reached out and caught it in midair. He looked at me, his eyes as big as saucers, jumped up, spun around, and slapped his hand on his leg. "Don't tell me God doesn't answer prayer!" he shouted. "You see, God is even interested in little things like trailer-hitch knobs and a kid's bicycle and little birds that die. Isn't that something?"

By then, I was in tears. "He sure does, Billy," I said. "And sometimes He also uses the foolish things of this world to confound the wise." We both got down on our knees then and really began to pray. Mine was a prayer of repentance. "Lord, forgive my stubbornness and lack of patience. And, Lord, help me never again to take the need for prayer lightly."

No great miracle was wrought that day, except in my heart. When I placed my hand on the trailer hitch, I evidently, by accident, depressed a pin in the hub of the turn knob—a safety pin that was designed to hold the ball joint in case the knob should accidentally loosen. Neither of us knew about it.

Sometime after the incident, I was sharing the story with Ruth Miner, a good friend from Virginia. She gave me the poem that is at the beginning of this chapter. Her mother had taught it to her as a little girl. I immediately memorized it and now quote it often as a constant reminder.

15
Duke Power Company Supplies Firewood

So do not worry, saying, "What shall we eat?" or "What shall we drink?" or "What shall we wear?" For the pagans run after all these things, and your heavenly Father knows that you need them. But seek first his kingdom and his righteousness, and all these things will be given to you as well (Matt. 6:31-33).

Not only did God show me how important prayer was to being fruitful in labor, but also how important it is to continually feed our spirit from His word.

Without realizing it, I had become so busy working on the camp during my off days from the airline that I began to neglect my daily Bible reading. And soon, everything started going wrong. I found myself spending more time working on the equipment than I did using it. At least half of my time seemed to be spent solving problems that caused me to work harder and read my Bible less. Then it dawned on me. My spiritual life was waning and growing anemic from a lack of feasting on God's Word.

So I decided to do something about it, regardless of what else was left undone. I was going to read my Bible. Getting up early the next morning, I put on a pot of coffee and made myself comfortable at the kitchen table. I was determined to fatten my spirit once again on God's Word. Later Charlotte got up and cooked breakfast for me and the girls. I ate with them, having a fork in one hand and the Bible in the other.

After breakfast when the girls left for school, Charlotte dressed and was ready to leave for a ladies' Bible study before

she interrupted me. "What are your plans for the day?" she
asked.

"My plans are to sit and read my Bible all day. I've neglected it
far too long," I told her.

"Well, you know winter is coming on, and there still hasn't
been any firewood cut. If we plan to use our fireplaces a lot this
winter, we're really going to need it," she said.

"I know," I said, "but right now, I feel this is more
important."

Around ten o'clock that morning, the telephone interrupted
my reading. "Hello, this is Duke Power Company calling," the
person on the other end of the line said. "We've noticed several
trees on your property that are beginning to interfere with our
lines, so with your permission, we'd like to cut them down."

"Sure," I said, "That's OK with me."

"What would you like for us to do with the wood?" the man
said.

"How about cutting it up into 24-inch lengths?" I asked.

"We'd be glad to," the voice said. "We'll start cutting just as
soon as the crew can get out there."

Around noon, Charlotte came back home. I was sitting in the
same position as when she'd left—still reading.

"Have you been sitting there all day?" she asked. It was apparent she was a little disgusted with me.

"Yes, I have hardly moved." I said as I glanced up. I knew
what her next question was going to be, and I couldn't wait to
tell her what happened.

"What about the firewo . . ." she started to say.

"Wait, wait," I held up my hand to stop her. "Don't worry
about it," I gloated. "Duke Power just called, and they have a
crew down in the pasture right now cutting it for us." Then I
began laughing as I told her what had happened.

"Oh, you!" she said as she threw her Bible study book at me.
Then we both cracked up laughing. We realized that God was
still teaching us His ways, and one of those ways was that regardless of what else may be screaming for our time, neglecting to
study His Word is not an option.

16
The Burning Rose Bushes

There the angel of the Lord appeared to him in flames of fire from within a bush. Moses saw that though the bush was on fire it did not burn up. So Moses thought, "I will go over and see this strange sight—why the bush does not burn up" (Ex. 3:2-3).

My episode with burning bushes wasn't exactly like that of Moses, but it was used by God just the same—to help drive home to me the importance of establishing proper priorities.

The building of our house had been almost completed, but the surrounding yard area was still in shambles. We'd cleared out a pine thicket to make room for the house, and the dead brush had been left piled up until we could get an opportunity to burn it. There was also a spindly hedgerow of pesky, wild rose bushes that separated our lot from our neighbor Virgil Womack's beautiful stand of white pines.

So we decided to get rid of the hedgerow first. Charlotte and I had spent hours for several days gingerly working in the thorns, tugging, digging, cutting, and trying to get rid of them. But for all our effort, we'd only managed to clear less than ten feet of the three-hundred-foot-long hedgerow. It was apparent that the task was going to be a long and tedious one. So we had set aside another of my few days off to tackle the job again. But just as I was getting ready to go out and begin that day, the telephone rang. It was our pastor from Salem Methodist, Reverend Fred Hill. Fred and I had gotten to be good friends, and he'd called to ask if I would go with him to visit some shut-ins. My first impulse was to tell him yes, but then the desire to get rid of those ugly rose bushes overrode my yes.

"Fred, I'm very sorry, but I have this important job that I just have to finish, maybe next time."

"Oh, that's OK," he said. "I'd love to have you go, but if you can't, I understand."

I was about to hang up when that soft little voice spoke up: "Seek ye first the kingdom of God, and His righteousness; and all these [other] things shall be added unto you" (Matt. 6:33, KJV). "Wait a minute, Fred!" I said, "I've changed my mind. Where should I meet you?"

When I hung up the phone, Charlotte who'd been listening, asked, "What's that all about?" And I explained to her how the remembrance of Matthew 6:33 had influenced me to change my mind.

"Just remember, though," she laughed, "those rose bushes are going to be waiting for you."

Fred and I had a wonderful time visiting several elderly shut-ins. And as I was driving home, I was feeling good about having gone. It was the afternoon when I arrived at the house—a beautiful afternoon, clear skies with rays of sunset forming on the horizon, perfectly calm, and not a breeze stirring. The first thing I noticed when I got out of the car was the large pile of pine brush. *What a perfect time for burning that brush pile,* I thought. So I went into the house, got some matches, and soon had myself a fire going. The brush was very dry, and I had the comforting feeling that in a few minutes it would all be burned away. As I stood gazing into the flames, leaning on a rake I'd brought just in case I needed it, suddenly a strong gust of wind darted in from the south. My neighbor's white pines lay just to the north.

I glanced upward. There wasn't a cloud in the sky, but the wind was catching the flames causing them to roar quickly into a torch headed directly toward the rose-bush hedge and the beautiful stand of white pines. Before I could even react, the rose bushes were on fire, and the flames were climbing two of the tallest and most beautiful white pines.

I yelled for Barbara and Cheryl, the only ones at home. They both came running out of the house carrying a bucket of water. We threw the water at the flames, but it only caused a flicker, and the fire raged back up again. I knew all hope was gone. I fell down on my knees and pleaded with God, "Please, stop the wind, put out the fire, do something, Lord! Please, please help us!"

And then, as suddenly as it had started, the wind stopped. The two torching pine trees went out, and nothing was left burning except the hedgerow. Even the limbs of the white pines that hung over the rose bushes weren't catching on fire. I watched unable to believe it as the rose hedge dissolved in flames. They burned from the road, where we had started to clear them, to the backside of our yard. Even though the hedgerow continued beyond our yard and on back through the woods, for reasons known only to God the fire stopped at the back edge of our yard. It just flickered out. In less than thirty minutes, I had watched the dreaded task of getting rid of the rose bushes accomplished. The only damage that had been done was to the two scorched white pines.

When I went to my neighbor and told him what had happened and offered to pay for the damages, he smiled and said, "Since it happened the way you explained, let's just wait and see what happens to the two trees. Maybe God will save them.

And God did save the trees. Within weeks, new needles were growing, and within a couple of months, the trees were as healthy as any in the forest. More important, however, was the dramatic lesson I learned about putting my Heavenly Father's business first. Because I saw firsthand that evening how well He could take care of my business afterward.

17

Year of Recession Brings Blessing

Cursed is the one who trusts in man,
who depends on flesh for his strength
and whose heart turns away from the Lord.
He will be like a bush in the wastelands;
he will not see prosperity when it comes.
He will dwell in the parched places of the desert,
in a salt land where no one lives.

But blessed is the man who trusts in the Lord,
whose confidence is in him.
He will be like a tree planted by the water
that sends out its roots by the stream.
It does not fear when the heat comes;
its leaves are always green.
It has no worries in a year of drought
and never fails to bear fruit (Jer. 17:5-8).

We were still in the recession of '74, the day I stood on the steps of Salem United Methodist Church talking to Mrs. Ester Cooper, a dear elderly lady of the church. "O. A.," she said, "I feel so sorry for you and Charlotte."

"Why is that, Mrs. Cooper?" I asked.

"Well," she said, "you're just getting started on your camp, and this recession has to hit; people can't afford to help you as they would like."

My first thought was: *She's right. People won't be able to help as much.* But then I remembered the bountiful ways in which the Lord had provided for our needs up to this point, like the tractor. My brother Doug had called me one day to tell me he'd heard on the radio that a neighbor of ours had a tractor for sale.

"All the man is asking for it is one hundred dollars, and the buyer to take the payments." So I jumped in my pickup and drove to the neighbors. He was out in the field plowing with the tractor when I arrived. It looked almost new, a '67 Ford 2000 with a diesel engine.

"It's seven years old but has low hours, and I've taken good care of it," he said. The payoff was $2,600.

When I asked him why he wanted to sell it, the farmer said, "To tell you the truth, I just don't need it. I've got two other larger tractors, and this one is more an added expense than anything else." But while I was standing there talking to the farmer, a tractor dealer showed up and immediately offered the farmer more than he'd been asking for the tractor if he'd sell it to him.

The farmer spit his tobacco juice into the freshly plowed field and looked over at the dealer. "What do you take me for? I'm an honest man, and this gentleman," he said, nodding toward me, "was here first. It's his choice—just for what I've been asking."

The dealer turned to me: "I'll give you six hundred dollars to get in your truck and leave."

"Sorry," I smiled. Without his knowing it, the man had shown me that God was still providing our needs.

"Mrs. Cooper," I said, suddenly remembering that she was still standing there on the church steps waiting for my comments. "You don't have to worry about the camp. Our trust is in God, and He doesn't have recessions. He'll provide."

I'd grown considerably in my faith and trust in God. He'd provided us with a development plan, a tax-exempt corporation, and more recently the tractor. So it was time for us to get to work, recession or no recession. We didn't have much money, but there was plenty we could do without money.

We started off by soliciting the free services of Harry Cherry and the Soil Conservation Service. They helped me survey out the waterline on our proposed nine-acre lake and a one-acre farm pond. Harry also drew up the plans for constructing the dams. Because of the size of the large dam, his drawings for it had to be submitted to the state engineer in Raleigh for approval.

Jim Sinclair, one of Harry's men, and I surveyed the waterline for the lake. We made our way through the woods and under-growth with Jim peering through his surveyor's scope and me holding the gauge pole and sticking little red flags in the ground when he said, "Mark it."

We were taking a breather once when Jim said to me, "I've surveyed the waterline for many lakes, but I've never seen such a natural shoreline for a constructed lake like this one. I can just see the water lapping up on the banks. It's almost like we could set the marker flags without surveying. You know, God must have intended for a lake to be here from the beginning of creation."

"You're probably right," I said to Jim. "I've been thinking the same thing." After the lake sites were surveyed, we also marked off the boundary that would need to be cleared for the area zoned for recreation.

Then Billy Ayers and I, along with the help of some other vol-unteers, began cutting and selling some of the pine trees for pulpwood, but it was soon obvious that it was going to take us forever to accomplish all the clearing that needed to be done. Then right on cue, God sent a pulp woodcutter, Willie Blanton. Willie usually only contracted for large tracts of timber. But I just happened to catch him when he had finished such a tract and was between jobs. He liked what I told him about our dream camp, so he agreed to begin clearing our trees right away.

With Willie working, we were getting the land cleared and generating some income as well—not much—but after all, we were working by faith—one step at a time.

About that time, I also met agent Gilmer Edwards of the ASCS, a government service to assist farmers and other rural folks. When I told him about our dream, Mr. Edwards offered his help. What I really needed was matching government funds through his office to help us build the lakes. But I'd already checked that out, and I knew it would be a waste of time to even mention this to him. So I politely thanked him for his offer and forgot about it.

Then a few weeks later, I got up one morning feeling so miser-able I could hardly stand myself. I told Charlotte that I needed to take a ride and climbed in my old pickup. The cab of that old

'70 Chevy often turned out to be my sanctuary. That was the case this particular morning. "Lord," I said. "I'm sure glad You don't have bad days like this, or we'd all be in trouble." Then I felt ashamed. "God, please forgive me for the way I'm acting. What I'd really like for You to do is take this day and somehow turn it around—make something beautiful happen for Your glory."

Then as clear as if I had heard it audibly, came these words: *Go up to the ASCS office and apply for the funds you need to help with the lakes.*

"But," I protested, "I've already been told that they don't have—have never had—funds available for helping to construct ponds." But then I remembered it was the Lord speaking to me. What did I have to lose by trying?

So I took off for Rutherfordton, our county seat, and walked into the ASCS office thirty minutes later. Mr. Edwards greeted me warmly. "O. A., what can we do for you?"

"Well, it's a little hard to explain, Mr. Edwards," I said. "What I'm going to tell you may sound a little crazy, but I've had a keen direction from God to come up here and apply for some assistance in building our lakes. Do you by any chance happen to have such funds available?"

"You know, O. A.," he said, "we've never had funds available before."

"Yes, I do know. That's what makes this whole thing sound so crazy. Wait a minute," I said, "that we've never had the funds before. You mean you do now?" I asked, my excitement growing.

"Well, yes and no. A lot of farmers have started canceling out on their cost-sharing programs because of the recession and their money being so tight. They're having difficulty coming up with their share of the cost. So this has left a small surplus in our budget, and because so many requests have been coming in over the years to help in constructing ponds, we've decided to use the surplus to help with those projects." He hastily added, "I have to tell you, all the funds that have been made available so far have already been applied for."

But nothing he could have said would have discouraged me by that time. My faith was growing by leaps and bounds. There were going to be more funds becoming available. I knew it. "Mr. Edwards, I believe it was God that led me up here, and I don't think He would have done that without a purpose. So if you'll just give me an application to fill out, I'll know that I've done my part," I told him.

"Sure, but I just don't want you to get your hopes up too high. Even if the money were to come available, only your small pond would qualify. The government would pay 60 percent of the cost," he explained.

"That would be a great help," I said. "And," I reached over and patted him on the back, "don't worry about me. I'll do my best and leave the rest to God."

He scratched his head for a moment and said, "Oh, there is one other thing I forgot to tell you. This program ends the first of November—all funded projects have to be completed by that time."

Boy, did that dash cold water on my faith. That only gave me two months! And we hadn't even started clearing the small pond site. It was at least a half mile from the nearest road, and the worst part was there was no way to get to it—not even an old logging road to get the pulpwood truck through. I laid down the pen I'd been using to fill out the application and was about to walk out when the Lord began to prompt my spirit: *Why do you think I would have brought you here if the job was impossible?* So I picked the pen back up.

My heart was telling me to fill out the application, and my mind was telling me it was a waste of time. But finally my spirit won out, and I filled out the form with the promise to Mr. Edwards that I would let him know if I changed my mind. After going home, I tried to figure all the angles, and I decided the most direct route to the pond site would be across our neighbor Virgil Womack's property. We had bought the pond site from Virgil, so I thought maybe he wouldn't mind letting us have a right-of-way across his remaining property.

Virgil was cordial toward my request. "I wouldn't mind your crossing my land, but there is probably a better way," he said. "If Grover Davis will permit you to cross his property from the other road, it'll be much closer."

Mr. Davis owned the property adjoining the east side of our property. But I'd gotten the idea that Mr. Davis was somewhat of a recluse who didn't like trespassers. But Virgil told me that Mr. and Mrs. Davis had both been sick and were staying over in Forest City with their daughter, Lucy Downey. I thanked him for his help and hung up the phone still not quite sure what to do.

But after a while, I began to feel adventuresome. I decided to drive up to the Davis home place and check things out. The road leading in was rough, not much better than an old wagon trail. Apparently, it hadn't been used much lately. When I finally got to the house, about a half mile from the main road, I found it grown up with tall grass and weeds. I parked my pickup and got out to look around a bit. Then I spotted what appeared to be an old logging road leading north through a grove of hardwood trees. I decided to hike up it and see where it led.

After walking for about two hundred yards, I came to a pine tree thicket that looked a little familiar, and a little further on I spotted a ravine, then a little red marker flag. "Wonder who in the world stuck that out here in the middle of nowhere," I mumbled as I stumbled along, pushing limbs out of my face. But then I spotted another and another. Suddenly I realized those red flags were the ones Harry Cherry and I had placed there months earlier. The old trail had led me right to the middle of the pond site! The Lord and I had a little celebration right there. I knew that He had been guiding my every step, and with my trusty tractor and bush hog, that old logging road could be opened up in no time at all.

Back home again, I still didn't know how I was going to approach Mr. Davis and convince him to let me have right-of-way across his land. Just the thought of having to ask scared me to death. So in order to deal with the fear, I began to pray. The Bible I'd placed on my lap opened to the twenty-eighth chapter of Job, but the only words my eyes focused on were the first words of verse 11, "He bindeth the floods from overflowing" (KJV). Wow! Fireworks went off in my spirit! How much clearer did God have to speak? I threw my Bible in the air and ran to the telephone. "There is no way Mr. Davis can refuse me," I kept telling myself as I dialed his daughter's number.

"Uh, uh, this is Captain Fish," I said, hoping the title might impress her a little. Right then, I couldn't think of anything else that might help.

"Oh! Captain Fish!" she said, "We've really been wanting to meet you."

"You, you've been wanting to meet me?" I asked puzzled.

"Yes sir!" she said. "I've been wanting to tell you how proud Mom, Dad, and I are about what's happened to Billy. We're so grateful to you!"

I couldn't figure out who she was talking about. "Billy who?" I asked.

"Billy Ayers!" she exclaimed.

Then it hit me. *Of course! Grover Davis was Billy Ayers' grandfather—the same Billy who was a part of the Hopewell Hoodlums.* I was so overwhelmed I could barely concentrate on what Lucy was saying.

But I finally made out, "What can we do for you? How can we ever repay you?"

When I was able to catch my breath, I told her I wanted to use their road while constructing the pond. "Of course," she replied. "Use it. Do anything you like with it. If I could, I'd give you the place!" So I thanked her and hung up, then immediately went down to where Willie was cutting trees at the big lake site. I told him I wanted him to start clearing the small lake site the next morning. When I explained to him the incredible story that was unfolding, he, too, was astounded. Then I got my tractor and within minutes the logging road was ready for use.

I was as excited as though the pond were already built, but I knew there were still two hurdles to cross: finding a construction contractor which wasn't busy and having the ASCS funds become available. I wasn't familiar with any contractors, so being in a hurry, I turned to the yellow pages. The ad for H & A Grading Company caught my attention. It stated among other things that they constructed ponds. When I called the number, Herman Sisk answered. I learned he was the "H" half of the company, and his father-in-law, Aden Epley, was the "A" half. Aden just happened to be an old flying buddy from back when I first started flying. As soon as I heard his name, I knew that God was again giving me favor with these guys.

Within a couple of days, Herman and Aden came to visit and look over the proposed site and talk about flying. They really wanted to help, but Herman said, "It'll be at least two months before we can get to you; we've got at least a half-dozen others ahead of you." I knew that would be too late, but for some reason, God seemed to be saying, "Stick with these guys."

Within a few days, I got a call from Mr. Edwards. "O. A.," he said, "I just wanted to let you know, some more money has become available, and although we're still a long way from getting to your application, I thought this news might encourage you a little."

It sure did, because that same day I got a call from Herman telling me that due to the recession a couple of their jobs had canceled. The same thing kept happening over the next few weeks. I was slowly moving up both lists. Meanwhile, each passing day was drawing us agonizingly closer to the deadline. Willie Blanton had already accomplished his part by clearing out all the trees, and all we could do was wait.

Finally, we were down to within three weeks of the deadline, the very minimum time Herman had said he'd need to complete the work. And I hadn't heard anything from him or Mr. Edwards for a couple of days. In fact, the last I'd heard from Herman was that we still had four ponds ahead of us on his list. But one afternoon, I got a call from Mr. Edwards. "Guess what?" he said. "We've finally gotten down to your name with about half of your funds available."

"Praise the Lord!" I shouted. "I'm believing that soon we'll have it all."

"That's fine," he said, "but you'll have to have the equipment on hand ready to start before we can credit the money to your account."

I had been fasting all day, and my heart was very tender toward God as I sat meditating on the back porch about four o'clock that afternoon. Then I thought I heard what sounded like a heavy tractor-trailer crawling up through the woods on the old logging road. But I knew sounds could be confusing with all the mountains and hollows around us. Soon, the droning of the truck engine died away with my sagging spirit. "Must have been a logging truck climbing Jackmore Mountain," I muttered.

But then a few minutes later, through the trees, came the spitting sound of a diesel Caterpillar engine roaring to life. A bulldozer was being unloaded at the pond site! I jumped off the porch and went running through the woods toward the sound. And I got there just in time to see Herman's smiling face as he parked the unloaded dozer. "Well, here we are," he said. "The rest of the equipment will be here in the morning, and we'll be ready to start."

"How did you manage to make it?" I asked, out of breath.

"Well, our few remaining customers agreed to let us put your work ahead of them," he told me.

When I told Mr. Edwards the good news about the dozer being there, he said. "I've got some more good news!" Your full share of funds is ready to be credited." Then laughingly added, "Let's just pray that it doesn't start raining and cause us to miss the deadline."

"It wouldn't dare," I responded.

And it didn't rain. With only a couple of days to spare, the pond we affectionately named the Dead Sea, even though it's brimming with blue gill and bass, was completed. Truly the words of the prophet Jeremiah had proven true. For like a tree planted by the waters in a period of recession, God had caused us to prosper.

(Top, left) Cheryl and Barbara sending their dad, O. A., off for his first flight as an airline pilot **(Top, right)** Barbara Jean in 1973 **(Bottom left)** Aunt Eddie and Uncle Frank on the steps of their farm house located on the property O. A. bought **(Bottom, right)** O. A.'s dad and mom, Otho, Sr., and Pauline Fish, with O. A.'s older brother, Eugene (Unless indicated otherwise, photos are the courtesy of O. A. Fish.)

(Top) Captain Fish at the controls of his DC-9 in 1973 **(Bottom)**
A family portrait taken not long after Barbara's death--left to right,
Kim, Lisa, O. A., Charlotte, and Cheryl

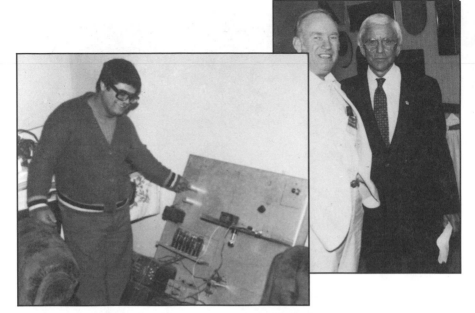

(Top, right) Captain Fish with George Otis, President and Founder of High Adventure Ministries **(Top, left)** Charbel Youness of South Lebanon pointing toward his homemade transmitter **(Bottom)** Captain Fish visiting with Major Haddad in his home

(**Top**) The Joy Center at South Mountains Christian Youth Camp (**Center**) Recent picture of the Billy Ayers family (left to right) Bill, his wife Beck, and their daughters Megan and Amanda (**Bottom**) The Fish "dream home"

(Top) Flight Attendant Barbara Armstrong and O. A. putting shingles on the roof of a cabin at South Mountains Christian Youth Camp **(Bottom)** Armored personnel carrier in front of Major Haddad's home

The magnificent painting by John Solie for *Reader's Digest* (September 1986) article "39,000 Feet Over Florida" (permission for *Reader's Digest* use was granted by *Guideposts* which published the original). Photo of painting courtesy of *Reader's Digest* and John Solie© 1986. Used by permission.

18

The Miracle of Johnny House and Two Pipes for One

I have planted, Apollos watered; but God gave the increase. So then neither is he that planteth any thing, neither he that watereth; but God that giveth the increase (1 Cor. 3:6-7, KJV).

The spring following construction of the small lake found us busily preparing for our first overnight campers. Charlotte had found some ladies to volunteer as counselors, and they had planned a weekend camp for girls. We were excited because that camp was to be the first fruits of years of hard labor.

The campsite situated on the southern slope of Cherry Mountain had a spectacular view overlooking the pond. Our church group had cleared out the undergrowth, a picnic shelter had been constructed from lumber sawed from our own trees, and the aluminum sheeting for its roof had been donated. We had also gathered several tents and a portable water container. So all we needed was an old-fashioned outhouse.

A friend had promised to bring his backhoe and dig the pit for me, but as the camping date neared, the friend had not appeared on the scene. I kept reminding God of His promise to raise up the expert help I needed, but nothing seemed to work. Finally, we had wearied to the point of having to cancel the camp.

"Lord, what are we going to do?" I begged.

His answer wasn't exactly what I wanted to hear: "You have a pick, shovel, and strong back. You also have the expertise to dig a pit, so stop complaining and go to work!"

My first thought was: *Surely this can't be God speaking,* but I thought in my heart it was. So I got my Bible to read while I was resting, my tape recorder to listen to God's Word while I was working, and my pick and shovel and headed for the campsite.

Digging the first two feet was easy. Then the hard-packed clay seemed to turn into concrete. Painful blisters on my hands soon joined an aching back to make the job even more miserable. I'd work for a while and rest for a while, and the whole time I was complaining, "Lord, if I have to build this whole camp with a pick and shovel, it's going to take a thousand years." But the Scripture from Romans 8:28 kept coming to mind: "We know that all things work together for good" (KJV). And I'd argue back, "What possible good can come from my digging a toilet pit by hand?"

By lunchtime on the second day of digging, I'd almost dug and chiseled my way to the proper depth for the pit. "How's it going?" Charlotte asked as we sat down to eat.

"Just about finished," I grunted without looking up.

"That's too bad," she said.

"Too bad!" I inquired. "What in the world do you mean, woman?"

"Well," she said, "Henry Glover, a neighbor whom you haven't met, called a while ago wanting to speak to you. When I told him where you were and what you were doing, he couldn't believe you were digging that toilet pit by hand. He said he has a backhoe and is free for a couple of hours each day at noon, and he would be delighted to help out."

Once again, God had been at work in the midst of my complaining. I felt so ashamed. Yet, He had used my willingness to dig the pit by hand to touch the heart of a man I had never met— a man with a backhoe. When I called Glover, he said, "Charlotte told me about you digging that toilet pit by hand. You shouldn't have to do that. I have a backhoe, and I'd be glad to donate it and my time to help."

Hurriedly I told him about another urgent job he could handle. The Old Grover Davis Road that led to the campsite was badly rutted and needed two drainage pipes installed to make it passable during rainy weather. Because of limited funds we had purchased only enough joints of concrete pipe to install one of them, and I needed at least one of them laid. Of course, you know Henry's answer.

"Sure, I can get that first thing tomorrow morning," Henry said.

Early the next morning, during prayer time I thanked God for sending Henry's willingness to help, and specifically prayed, "Lord, I want you to cause our efforts to prosper today—double what we would normally accomplish."

Henry was there waiting for me. In fact, he had already measured the width of the road and calculated that I needed another joint of pipe. "If you'll go get the pipe, I'll dig the ditch while you're gone, O. A.," he suggested. "Then we'll be ready to put it in by the time you get back." Just as an afterthought, I told him about my prayer that morning—asking God to double our productivity for the day.

When I got back with the pipe, I noticed that Henry had dug the drainage portion of the ditch but had stopped when he reached the lower edge of the road. I couldn't figure out what was going on. He was simply sitting on his backhoe, seemingly daydreaming. I said, "What's wrong? You have a breakdown?"

"Nope," he answered. "Nothing's wrong."

When I gave him a "well-then-what-the-heck-are-you-sitting-there-for" look, he climbed down from his tractor and said, "Come over here," and pointed to the edge of the road where he had stopped digging. I still couldn't see what he was pointing to, so he said, "Jump down into the ditch." When I did, I saw that directly under the road, right in the center of the ditch Henry had dug, was a fifteen-inch concrete pipe that had been buried there a long, long time. Before Henry had started digging, there was absolutely no sign that a pipe had ever been there. "If you'll notice," said Henry, "It's only half filled with dirt. I'll open the other end, and the first big rain will clean it out."

All I could do for the moment was stand there and thank God for His faithfulness. Then I told Henry about the other location up the road where we needed another pipe installed. Within another hour that one was also completed. God had given the increase. Afterwards, all Henry could do was shake his head and smile.

The weekend the camp opened, I came home from a flight. As I anxiously walked toward the shelter where Charlotte and her counselors were taking a break, a little girl came running down the hill toward me. Suddenly a consuming feeling of love for that child swept over me. I knew as I held out my arms to her that it was Jesus' love I was feeling, and, in essence, my arms were His arms hugging her. And I remembered the words with which he had first called me, "let the little children come unto me."

When I arrived at the shelter, I told Charlotte what had happened. "I don't know who that little girl is, but I do know that God has a very special love for her." Then I learned she was a foster child of our special friends, Sharon and Tinnin Wilson. Her real father had deserted the family, and she'd been taken from an alcoholic mother. So from that day forward, I've learned to be sensitive to that special kind of love and willing to be used as an instrument to pass it on to His hurting children.

Truly He is the God who gives the increase, whether we are digging toilet pits, planting drainage pipes, or passing out His love.

19
Tested By Fire

His work will be shown for what it is, because the Day will bring it to light. It will be revealed with fire, and the fire will test the quality of each man's work (1 Cor. 3:13).

Up to this phase of the camp's supernatural growth, a certain pattern revealing God's fingerprints had emerged without my recognizing it. A time of testing always preceded each recognizable divine intervention of the camp's construction. And the next phase was to be no different.

We had our fish pond and a primitive campsite, but our recreation area was nothing but stumps and piles of brush. We didn't even have a cleared level space big enough to play ball. Willie had finished cutting over the large lake site and the zoned recreational area. But after that, we hadn't known what to do. Grading out a ball field, tennis court area, parking lot, and the camp's main entrance road would require carving up a dome-shaped knoll and filling in some pretty deep ravines. I had figured the construction cost for all this wouldn't be available anytime soon.

However, my impatience wouldn't allow me to sit around and do nothing. I decided that if I was very careful, I could burn some of the brush piles in the cut-over area. That would be some progress at least. It was fall, the leaves had all dropped, and it hadn't rained in a long time the day I decided to start burning the selected brush piles. It was so powdery dry that I still don't understand why the fire service issued me a burning permit, but they did. I knew it was hazardous, but I had only so many days off and besides, I told myself, "I'll be very careful; I'll only burn a couple of the safer piles."

But when I lit a match to the brush, flames leaped into the air as though it had been soaked in gasoline. It was scary, but I still wasn't too worried. I had cleared out the brush piles well and figured I was pretty safe. And in a few minutes they had burned down to nothing more than a good-sized camp fire and seemed harmless enough, so I decided to get ready to go home for lunch. But just as I was leaving, a twig snapped within one of the fires and went flying through the air like a flaming pinwheel, landing in the middle of another brush pile that was a good fifty feet away.

It immediately exploded into flames, reaching hungrily toward a stand of hardwood trees nearby. I panicked when I saw the carpet of leaves under the trees which was at least a foot thick. I grabbed a rake and started working like crazy trying to build a fire lane to keep the flames from spreading into the woods. I knew if it did, and a little wind came up, the whole mountain and camp could be burnt to a crisp.

Within seconds the flames had jumped my breakline, and the woods were on fire. I yelled at the top of my lungs for help and raked as hard as I could to try to establish another breakline, all the time praying that help would arrive. Luckily a man camping out on the Grover Davis place heard my yelling and saw the smoke. He came on the run, grabbed a rake, and started helping to clear the breakline, but it was futile. The fire jumped the lanes as fast as we could build them. Finally, Charlotte, smelling smoke, turned off the lawn mower she was operating, heard our cries for help, and called the fire department. Over the next twenty minutes, four different volunteer fire units arrived. With the woods full of men and trucks fighting the fire, after about an hour, except for some smoldering stumps in the burnt area, the fire was out. A couple acres of hardwood trees and a good portion of the cleared-out area had burned.

When I got home after the fire was out, I collapsed into my recliner totally exhausted. I had never exerted so much energy in my life. And it all started because of my impatience. So while recovering from the fiery ordeal, I spent much time in prayer and meditation, seeking God's direction for my next move. One thing for sure, I wasn't ready to run out and set more brush piles on fire. At least not until we could hire a bulldozer to clear a wide firebreak lane all around the clear-cut area that still needed to be burnt. I wasn't about to take any more chances with the camp and woods.

So I called Herman Sisk once again to ask for his help. "O. A.," he said. "I'm terribly sorry, but we're building roads for the state now, and we're booked solid for the next two years. We'd love to be able to construct your ball field, big lake, and everything, but I just don't know when or if we'd ever be able to get to it."

"Herman," I tried to sound confident, "don't worry about us. I've learned a little something about patience lately, and when it's God's timing, you'll have the time, and we'll have the money."

He laughed and said, "Maybe."

Amazingly enough, however, we didn't have to wait long for God to move. That spring I got a call from Herman. "How would you like to get that ball field built?"

I was too flabbergasted to speak for a moment. "What do you mean get the ball field built?" I asked. "We don't have the money to do it."

"Well, I have an offer you can't refuse. All I'm asking is that you pay my men's salary and the operating cost of the equipment—about twenty bucks an hour, maybe less."

I couldn't believe my ears. "What's happening? Just a few months ago, you said you were booked up for two years."

"Yeah, but the state's run out of money for this fiscal year and canceled all contracts until after the new fiscal year starts in July. My men need work." He laughed and then added, "Plus our church softball team needs a field to use. That's all I'm asking in return. Just let us use the field for playing some of our home games." He was right. It was a deal I couldn't refuse. Even though we didn't have much money, there was no doubt that this deal, too, had been planned by God, and I was confident He would meet the need.

Within days, two big bulldozers, three earth moving pans, and a motorgrader were hard at work, pushing brush up into huge burning piles, digging up stumps, and moving dirt around. As soon as it was cleared, Harry Cherry came out and surveyed the ball field, the parking lot, and roadway. Over the next few weeks, the face of the whole landscape changed. With the little money that we had saved plus what Charlotte and I could contribute, we were able to pay within $10,000 of the total bill, and even that was paid within a few months. Over $40,000 worth of grading had been accomplished for less than half the normal cost.

But since God had worked it out I knew there would be more blessings in store. And after finishing the recreation area, Herman said that he still had enough time to build our big lake before going back to building roads. The only problem was the approval for constructing the dam was being held up in the state engineer's office in Raleigh. No amount of prodding seemed to hurry them along, and each trip to my mailbox brought more disappointment. Our time was growing agonizingly short those days, and my faith was once again being tested, but I should have known by then that God had another adventure in the making.

20

An Adventure of Faith

"Have faith in God," Jesus answered. "I tell you the truth, if anyone says to this mountain, 'Go, throw yourself into the sea,' and does not doubt in his heart but believes that what he says will happen, it will be done for him" (Mark 11:22-23).

Uncle Frank and Aunt Eddie were particularly proud of what was happening with the property they'd been instrumental in helping me buy from M. D. Harrill. Uncle Frank would often say, "Boy, O. A., I wish Dee had lived long enough to see what you are doing with his farm."

Almost every day, Frank would walk up to where Herman and his men were moving dirt around and watch for hours. He could hardly wait for us to get started constructing the dam for our big lake. Our own Lake Galilee was to be built practically in his backyard, and it was designed to catch the fresh water of two spring-fed brooks that flowed by his house. The backdrop would also provide a cozy nook for their home which would be backed by the dam and bordered on both sides by rolling wooded hills.

But just before the ball field was finished, Uncle Frank died of a sudden heart attack. After the funeral, I visited Aunt Eddie to offer her whatever comfort I could. I sat at the kitchen table as she fumbled with a pan of steamy biscuits right from her wood stove. "I don't know what I'm going to do," she sighed.

"Do about what?" I asked. The aroma of hot bread brought back memories of happier times and the scrumptious country dinners Aunt Eddie used to bake when mom and dad would take us to visit her and Uncle Frank.

"I really don't want to move from here," she said interrupting my thoughts. "But with Frank gone, I can't afford the rent anymore."

"Don't worry, Aunt Eddie," I whispered in her ear while slipping my arm around her frail shoulders. "This house is yours for as long as you want it, and you don't have to worry about the rent."

I felt good as I made my way home through the pine forest that separated our houses. It was a warm summer day. The rich smell of pine resin tickled my nose as I strolled along the path kicking up pine needles. There had been doubts when I first felt God leading us back to this spot, but with the warm sun on my back and Aunt Eddie settled safely in her home, it all seemed so right. If the plans for the dam would just hurry up and come so we could get started on it, everything would be perfect.

I swung by the mailbox on my way home. Maybe the plans for the dam would be there. "We're on our way!" I shouted as I spotted the large manila envelope with a Raleigh return address on it. I raced home, bounded up the steps of our foyer, and eagerly ripped open the envelope. Then spread the plans out on the kitchen table. That's when I spotted the hand-scrawled note on the plans. It read, "House below dam site will have to be removed." My stomach knotted, and my knees went weak as I slumped into a nearby chair. "Aunt Eddie's house," I moaned as the sickening thought of tearing it down hit me. "God, why did you let this happen? Everything was going so well."

I paced back and forth across the kitchen trying to sort out the confusion. Doubt in everything I'd come to believe pounded at me. In desperation, I prayed, "Lord, help me. I want to believe, but, Lord, right now I can't."

Then seemingly out of nowhere the Bible verse Mark 11:23 began to run through my mind, "I tell you the truth, if anyone says to this mountain, 'Go, throw yourself into the sea,' and does not doubt in his heart." Suddenly it dawned on me, it didn't say anything about doubting with my mind. Nowhere in the Bible did it instruct me to believe with my mind. It was as though I could hear God saying to me, "Son, I know about your doubts, but My faith which is given to you comes from a source that doubts cannot reach—your heart."

Almost before I could ask the question: "What can I do about my doubts?" the verse from Mark 11 continued: "But believes that what he says will happen, it will be done for him." God was telling me I couldn't let those doubts control me, but instead I should confess from my heart my continuing confidence and trust in Him. I had to tell others about my confidence and trust in Him even though my mind might still be doubting.

I went into the living room where Charlotte was reading the paper and, without saying a word, showed her the plans, pointing out the engineer's note. A startled look came over her face. "What in the world are we going to do?" she asked.

"I don't know, but I believe," I said as I stood up straight and started again. "I believe with all my heart that God will give us the solution for this problem."

But showing the plans to Charlotte was not enough. For some reason I felt like I also had to share the problem with Herman Sick who was working down on the ball field. When I walked up to where Herman was standing, all the other men shut down their equipment and came over. It was as though God was drawing an audience for the speech I was about to deliver.

Herman's reaction was the same as Charlotte's and mine when I showed him the note. "What are we going to do, O. A.?" he asked, "You know we don't have any time to waste."

"I don't know, Herman, but I believe with all my heart that God is going to provide a solution for our problem," I told him. Herman and all his men looked dejected as I walked away.

I didn't feel much better as I stumbled up the newly graded entrance road on my way home, still struggling with lingering doubts. The only thing I noticed was the dirt clods I was kicking as I walked along, but I jerked back to reality as a pickup truck braked beside me. It was Harry Cherry. "How's it going, O. A.?" he asked.

"Just fine," I lied barely acknowledging the gentleman in the truck with him.

"Good," he said. "How about jumping in back and come help us run a gradient on the ball field? I think we're getting pretty close to our grade." I did as he asked and didn't even mention the altered plans for the dam until we had finished running the grid on the ball field. Then I pulled them out of my back pocket and spread them out on the hood of his truck. When I pointed to the engineer's note, I was surprised to find Harry wasn't reacting at all the way I'd expected him to. Instead, he was standing there smiling. Then he broke into a wide grin and nodded toward the man with him. "Why don't you ask this fellow about it. He's the engineer who wrote it."

I was too stunned to speak. Strange sensations raced up and down my spine. I tried to remain calm on the outside, but waves of praise and adoration to God for His faithfulness gushed up inside me. I knew that everything was going to work out—even before I spoke to the engineer.

Finally after regaining my composure somewhat, I told him about my Uncle Frank dying and my Aunt Eddie who was left living alone in the house and the vow I'd just made to her. "But the only reason I added the note," explained the engineer, "was because it looked like the water would flow right toward the house. Your plans didn't show a diversion for the overflow water that would go out your spillway, so I assumed you were planning to move it."

"Oh, no," I said as Harry shook his head. We've planned a terraced diversion that will carry the water beyond the house."

"I just didn't think it necessary to include the diversion in the construction plan for the dam," Harry added.

I watched speechlessly as the engineer took his pen and with one stroke cast my mountain into the sea, then I looked down at my watch. It had only been two hours since I'd met with Aunt Eddie. It would have taken the engineer four hours to drive from Raleigh to Rutherford County. This dramatic lesson on the heart kind of faith had been scripted by God, just for me, hours before I'd decided to visit my newly widowed aunt.

21
Pulp Woodcutter
and Address Labels

Therefore being justified by faith, we have peace with God through our Lord Jesus Christ: By whom also we have access by faith into this grace wherein we stand, and rejoice in hope of the glory of God. And not only so, but we glory in tribulations also: knowing that tribulation worketh patience; And patience, experience; and experience, hope: And hope maketh not ashamed; because the love of God is shed abroad in our hearts (Rom. 5:1-5, KJV).

At last, our Lake Galilee was under construction. It was thrilling watching Herman work his bulldozer in the bottom of the long, deep trench we'd cut to provide a solid core for the dam. Stretching out over five-hundred feet in length, the dam would eventually reach from one hillside to the other and would be thirty feet high in the center.

Herman saw me watching and crawled his dozer up out of the trench and over to where I was standing. "O. A.," he said, "Those big pine trees behind you are going to have to go."

I looked around at the twenty or more big, tall pines, horrified. "Why is that?" I asked. "I thought we had cleared the trees back plenty."

"But we're going to have to bulldoze up into them in order to tie in this end of the dam," he said.

"How much time do I have to get them cut?" I asked.

"None, really," he answered. "We'll need to be working there no later than tomorrow morning."

"But I don't know of anyone we could get on such short notice to come in and harvest them," I said.

"Well, it'd be better to just bulldoze them down and bury them out of our way rather than delay us," he told me.

The thought of wasting the marketable timber from those beautiful trees sickened me. However, I knew Herman was right. Their value was not worth holding up the men. Besides it was already noon, and within a couple of hours I was going to have to be dressed and on my way to Atlanta for a three-day flight. There seemed to be no hope of salvaging the trees.

"Let me go home and pray about it," I said to Herman. "I'll have an answer for you before I leave for work."

When I got home, Charlotte had lunch on the table. As we ate, I told her about the fate of the pine trees. "I know how you feel," she said. "All morning I've been praying for some address labels to help speed up a mailing I'm working on. Having to type the address on each envelope is wasting so much time."

"Honey," I said, "I guess we're just going to have to continue trusting God and doing the best we can. He knows about our needs." Our conversations was interrupted by the front doorbell. As I was going to answer it, the telephone started ringing, and Charlotte went to answer the phone. Standing at the front door was a frail-looking young man who was nervously twisting a ball cap in his hands.

"Are you Mr. Fish?" he asked.

"Yes, I am. What may I do for you?" I answered.

"Somebody told me you might have some wood I could cut," the man said.

I looked past him at an old pulpwood truck he'd parked in my drive. A shabbily dressed young woman sat in the truck holding a young baby in her lap.

"I really do need to earn some money," he said.

"You just wait right here for a minute," I told him as I turned and ran back up the steps to get my hat and tell Charlotte about the miracle on our front-door steps. But when I peeked into the dining room where she was standing at the telephone, she put her hand over the mouthpiece and said, "You'll never guess what this phone call is about. This lady has called to ask me if I could use some address labels. She has several thousand that she doesn't need."

"Wait until I tell you who is at the door!" I exclaimed.

We both just stood looking at each other laughing and crying at the same time. It was like we'd just received a love letter from God. All the trials, tests, and heartbreaks that had accompanied our victories suddenly seemed worth it. God was giving us His stamp of approval.

I led the young man and his wife down to the lake site and pointed out the trees that needed to come out, and I left him earning the much-needed cash for his family while Charlotte and I took a moment to bask in the knowledge of knowing that what we were doing was pleasing to our Heavenly Father.

22

Joy Center

Religion that God our Father accepts as pure and faultless is this: to look after orphans and widows in their distress and to keep oneself from being polluted by the world (Jas. 1:27).

The stories about South Mountain Christian Camp up to this point have primarily dealt with God's divine guidance and intervention during the initial development stages of the camp, but His help didn't stop there. It has continued throughout. I am convinced, however, that seeing God's hand so readily has had little to do with any great faith that Charlotte and I might have, but rather it's because of the ministry that He had called us to perform—a ministry of caring for God's little "orphans." We have discovered that today's society has produced a generation of "orphans" who have both parents living. Divorce, alcoholism, drugs, and lust for money are among the major factors that have created these orphans—kids who for the most part are left to defend themselves and to deal with deep emotional wounds that they're not capable of handling. God is raising up ministries like ours to apply His healing balm of Gilead to these young victims—victims of an adult generation that seems to have gone crazy.

It is this love for these special kids that continually motivates us. I say "special kids" because the majority of the kids we serve are termed, due to the lack of a better word, "disadvantaged." They are referred to us by social agencies and organizations, school counselors, churches, and just plain concerned citizens who are in a position to know about them. Over 60 percent of our campers return from previous seasons.

To accommodate the ministry, God has provided us with growth in facilities. In addition to our fish pond—the Dead Sea—and the sparkling waters of our Lake Galilee, we have two campsites with rustic cabins for housing the campers, bathhouses with hot and cold water to keep them clean, and a charming old brick farmhouse that has been renovated into our cafeteria. God has also provided picnic shelters, the ball field, other recreational areas, and hiking trails. He has also made provision for future expansion. The camp now covers over 250 acres. Part of that is the Old Grover Davis place. Lucy Downey, Billy Ayers' aunt, made possible the purchase of this land after her parents' died. That charming old farmhouse that is now our cafeteria is her old home place.

But there was one thing that we desperately lacked—good indoor facilities for chapel and recreation. One summer a few years ago, it rained almost every day for our six weeks of resident camps. The campers and counselors were suffering terribly from cabin fever. They soon ran out of ideas for indoor games. This bothered me greatly, and I made it an object of intense prayer.

Money from United Way, social agencies, civic clubs, Christian organizations, and concerned individuals was coming in to help cover the camper's cost, but funds for capital improvements were almost nothing. We had a few thousand dollars saved that had been donated for a memorial to honor our daughter Barbara who was killed in the auto accident. That was the total sum of our savings account.

It was in December, following the rainy season, and we were still without ideas or money when I picked up the funny paper one Sunday morning. I seldom read the funnies, but that day I began reading one of the cartoons. In this particular cartoon, the character was praying for God to help him win a lottery. Each day he picked up the newspaper and noticed that his name wasn't among the winners, and each day he asked, "Why God, why?"

In the last caption, God spoke to the character and said, "Give me a chance and buy a ticket." For me the punch line was amusing, but more than that, God used it to speak to me. He was saying to my heart, "A 100 percent of zero is zero. Give Me something to work with, and I'll provide your building for you." I became very excited because I knew that God had spoken to me.

Now Charlotte and I had put back a little money for emergency use only. Under specific guidance of God's Holy Spirit—and I want to emphasize that advisedly—I took the savings and invested it.

I was so sure this inspiration was from God that I immediately started looking at building contractors. God led me to Atchley Construction Company. Doug Atchley, the owner of the company, and his apt secretary, Joyce, were two of the most delightful people I had ever met. They even took me seriously when I told them I was depending on God to supply the money for the building. We signed a contract to build a 65- by 125-foot, insulated, steel building for $65,000, and I signed with only the small amount of money in the memorial fund on hand.

By late August the following year, God had multiplied my modest investment by several hundredfold. It was enough so that it enabled Charlotte and me to make a contribution to the camp, and when added to the memorial fund, the additional funds enabled us to pay cash for the building when it was completed a couple months later.

If there was one word that summed up Barbara's life, that word would be *joy*. So that's how the building got it's name: "Joy Center." It has become just that—the center of joy for our camping program. In it we have room for chapel, crafts, basketball, volley ball, and a thousand other games that the campers come up with. The gym section has four large, roll-up garage-type doors that, when opened, give the gym an open-air atmosphere. Not only does it protect the kids from the rain, but the gym also protects them from the intense summer heat which we sometimes experience.

Even more recently, through another government-sponsored cost-sharing program, we were able to build a three-section Ropes Challenge Course—a group initiative course, a low ropes, and a high ropes course. This fantastic course enables us to help instill into the kids self-esteem, trust, confidence, communication skills, reasoning, the ability to deal with fear, and many other attributes. It has been one of the greatest tools God has yet provided. Another good thing about the ropes course is that it has enabled us to work directly with the schools of our area, developing a relationship that's beneficial to all.

We are now capable of handling up to sixty children a week for seven weeks each summer. Our faith and trust in God is that our capacity will continue to grow.

Our earthly reward for all the hard work it takes to oversee this ministry, of course, is a continuous stream of positive reports telling of changed lives. Thousands of youngsters have made their decisions to accept Jesus as Lord here at camp, and hundreds have been baptized in our Lake Galilee.

Part 3:
Fullness of Witnessing

But you will receive power when the Holy Spirit comes on you; and you will be my witnesses in Jerusalem, and in all Judea and Samaria, and to the ends of the earth (Acts 1:8).

In Part 3, I have selected a few of the many stories of how God opened the doors of opportunity for me to witness. After receiving the anointing touch of God's power one night in an Atlanta motel room, I began to witness more and more about the Christ who dwelled within me. I became a witness to my family first, then to my peers and passengers at Eastern Airlines, to group meetings in the United States, and then to the Middle East where I became involved with High Adventure's Voice of Hope radio ministry in South Lebanon. The Lord has opened doors for me to minister on radio and national television and, finally, to minister through my writing.

23

Fifty-Seven-Dollar-
and-Fifty-Cent Opel

My God will meet all your needs according to his glorious riches in
Christ Jesus (Phil. 4:19).

My wife and daughters were the first to notice after I received
God's witnessing power. For the first time in my life, I was able
to openly talk about God and pray with them. But it wasn't that
easy with all my relatives.

I had a tremendous burden for my brother Eugene, but I still
had trouble witnessing to him. He was a wholesale used-car buyer in the D.C. area. After our daughter Barbara was killed in the
car accident, I was bumped out of Atlanta and back to Washington as a crew base. So since I still elected to commute from our
North Carolina home, I had to spend many nights in Washington. And many times, I would have to go up a day early for a
flight, or I would get in from a flight too late for a commute
home, so I spent most of those nights with Eugene.

He believed in God, but I knew it was going to take some special happening to get his attention before I could effectively talk
to him about Christ. And after seeking God's help in the matter,
I was impressed upon to involve Eugene in being the answer to a
specific prayer request of mine. I needed an inexpensive airport
car for Washington. I used my Chevy pickup to drive to the
Charlotte Airport where I caught the Eastern flight for my commute, but I didn't have a vehicle to drive while I was in the D.C.
area. So I had been praying for one.

Taking a big step of faith, I said, "Eugene, I've asked God to supply me a car, and I believe He's going to give it to me through you."

"Sure," he said. "I'll be happy to help you find a car. Just what kind do you want, and how much do you want to pay?"

"You don't understand," I said. "I've asked God to 'give' me a car. It doesn't matter what kind it is as long as it'll run."

Then I explained to Eugene how Charlotte and I had been donating all our nonessential resources to the camp. He appreciated our generosity in giving to the camp, but his expression said he was very skeptical about God providing me a car for free. "No, I don't know how God is going to supply this car, but I know that He is, and I believe that He is going to use you to bring it about. All I want you to do is keep alert to that fact. That's all I ask, just keep alert. Because He is going to do it."

A few days later I was sitting alone in the motel room while Eugene was out buying when the telephone rang. "Little brother," he said, "I haven't found a free car yet, but I've found one that's almost free."

"How's that?" I asked.

"I've got a little Opel sedan that I picked up for fifty dollars sight unseen. A very upset man just walked into the dealership here and wanted to trade it in. He said the clutch was gone, and he couldn't drive it. I gave him fifty dollars for it without even looking at it." He went on to tell me that it was sitting at a service station just blocks from the motel.

"Take a look at it," he said, "and if you want it, it's yours; but if not, I'm sure I can sell it."

I wasn't exactly comfortable with this situation. It was going to cost me $50 plus whatever it would take to fix the clutch, but I'd told Eugene God was going to give me a car for free. It was a bargain, that was for sure, but not the kind of answered prayer needed to be a real witness to Eugene.

The service station where the car was located was also adjacent to the old neighborhood where I'd lived before moving to North Carolina, so I called Bill Will, one of my neighbor friends, and asked him to pick me up and go with me. He knew a lot about cars, and I knew he'd be glad to help me.

The Opel was a nice-looking little car, good paint job, no

dents, the upholstery was almost like new, and it only had about 70,000 miles on the odometer. The only problem was that when the clutch was pushed, nothing happened. But Bill really liked it. "O. A.," he said, "you and I can put a clutch in it for less than a hundred dollars." So I took the car. I steered it while Bill pushed me in his car the few blocks to his house, and I decided to come up a day early for my next flight so we could work on it. But when I got back to Washington the next time, it was pouring rain, and Bill had discovered that it would take metric tools to work on the car which he didn't have. So I decided to call a mechanic I'd known in Alexandria since I needed the car as soon as possible.

Bill finally convinced me that we could drive the car in to the garage and save a $40 tow bill. "There's nothing to it," he said. "You drive my car, and I'll drive the Opel; you'll just have to stay right behind me. When I have to stop, I'll kill the engine. I'll put it in second gear, you can push me to get started, and I'll just keep going." Knowing how heavy the traffic can get, I was a bit anxious

But we decided to take the risk. We headed north on Route 1 toward town. Everything seemed to be going fine—until we stopped at the third traffic light. Instead of getting the Opel into second gear, Bill put it in reverse. When I started pushing him, the Opel began jumping up and down. Bill started frantically waving his arm out the window, and after a few yards I stopped pushing until he got it in second and gave me the go-ahead signal again.

Then when we came to Alexandria, traffic really began to pick up. At the next traffic light, Bill went through, but I got caught with the red light. I could see a number of cars pulling onto the highway behind the Opel, and I just knew we were going to end up getting a ticket for creating a traffic jam. The red light seemed to hold me for an eternity. Then I saw Bill making a left turn about two blocks ahead. "Help us, Lord," I prayed as I made the same left turn. But I didn't see him anywhere.

Then suddenly he zipped out in front of me from a side parking space. He was shouting something, so I rolled down the car window to hear him, "It's working!" he yelled. "It's working!"

"What's working?" I yelled back. But he just kept going and stopped a few blocks later in front of the garage. My mechanic friend came out as Bill excitedly explained how when he'd instinctively pushed the clutch pedal in after losing me at the red light, it had started working right, and it had been working ever since.

"Something must have jarred it loose," the mechanic said. "These clutches are bad to stick if they've been left sitting for a while." Bill and I both began to laugh. We knew that it had happened when he got it in reverse instead of second gear. We also knew this happening was no accident.

Everything else was working fine, so I took it to a service station and had the oil changed and a grease job. The cost was $7.50. When Eugene came home that evening and heard what happened, he just laughed and shook his head. "Well, $57.50's almost like nothing, but I was so sure that God was going to get it for me for free," I said.

"Don't you think that's asking God for a little much?" Eugene said.

"Maybe you're right," I answered, but I still wasn't sure.

When I got to work the next morning, I checked my mailbox in the crew mail room. There was a note there to get in touch with the flight operation's accountant. He informed me that I had not turned in a moving expense voucher for my transfer from Atlanta to Washington. I explained to him that I had not incurred any additional expense since I hadn't moved my household. "But we still owe you mileage expense for moving your car," he said. "But I didn't move a car."

"It doesn't matter," the accountant laughed. "Everybody gets that."

"But I don't know the mileage," I said.

"Oh, that's OK. We'll just use the suggested AAA mileage and leave a check in your mailbox.

When I got back from my flight a few days later, there was a check in my mailbox for $57.50. Eugene couldn't believe it when I got to the motel and showed it to him.

When Eugene passed away not long ago, this miracle came to my mind, and I thought, *I imagine that Jesus and Eugene are laughing about the $57.50 Opel right now.*

24
Launching Out By Faith

For God did not give us a spirit of timidity, but a spirit of power, of love and of self-discipline (2 Tim. 1:7).

Not long after Barbara was killed, I was sitting in the living room one evening thinking about how temporary life really was and how foolish we often are to let phobias rob us of living out our years to the fullest. I was especially concerned with how I had let fear hinder me from being the witness I'd wanted to be for God.

The thought ran through my mind: *I'm going to launch you out to testify for me.* Panic gripped me as I thought about the possibility of standing behind a church pulpit some day. I'd gotten to the point where I could share on an individual basis, but I was still apprehensive about standing before a crowd of people. And I didn't dare let myself think about speaking from a pulpit. I was afraid that I'd stand up and not be able to think of anything to say or that I'd become too emotional to speak. "Please, Lord," I prayed. "Don't put me behind a pulpit."

And the words seemed to come back to me, "You'll never get an opportunity to speak on My behalf, unless I give you the words. If I do give you an opportunity, it's because I have confidence in you, and if I have confidence in you, why should you be afraid?"

"Lord, when You put it like that," I said, "it doesn't sound so frightening. I'm going to trust You not to let anyone ask me to speak unless it's of Your doing. That way I'll know to accept the invitation."

It was less than two hours after this conversation with God

that the first opportunity came. A gentleman from Hopewell United Methodist Church called. "Captain Fish, our little Methodist men's group was wondering if you'd come and speak at our next men's fellowship breakfast. We meet the second Saturday of each month."

That was two weeks away, and butterflies were already settling in as the man continued to explain, "We usually only have about a half a dozen men show up, so I don't know if you'd want to bother coming for such a small group. I'm sure you're used to speaking to large groups." Little did he know that his would be my first group ever. And the fact that the meeting would be a small one told me that, indeed, this first opportunity was from God. It was His gentle way of easing me into His calling.

As I waited for the big day to arrive, I sweated over what I was going to say to the men. My wastebasket filled with notes as I started over and over again trying to write just the right message. But nothing appropriate seemed to come to mind. Finally, the night before I settled on some notes out of sheer desperation. I wasn't satisfied, but I knew they'd have to do.

The church was only a short distance from my home, so I arrived about ten minutes early. I could smell country ham frying as I walked into the fellowship hall. At least a dozen men greeted me with handshakes, hugs, and good wishes, and, in spite of the butterflies, I began to feel at home. I went light on the grits, biscuits, scrambled eggs, and country ham, but I stayed busy passing the platters back and forth to the hungry men.

Then finally after the tables were cleared and the chairs huddled, I heard myself being introduced. *This is it,* I thought, *my first speaking engagement.* I fought off the panic, and I about died as I knocked over my chair getting up to approach the podium. My mouth felt like cotton as I thanked the men for inviting me. But soon interesting thoughts began coming to my mind, and before I knew what was happening the men were hanging on my words. I had journeyed so far from my prepared notes that I folded them inconspicuously and slipped them into my back pocket. For the first time in my life I was experiencing the anointed word of God flowing through me, and it felt good.

I don't remember what I talked about, but it seemed to bless the men, and I was ecstatic that a barrier had finally been broken for me. That morning was the beginning of what has turned out to be hundreds of opportunities to share my love for God and faith in His Son, Jesus Christ. I had stepped out in faith, and God hadn't disappointed me.

25
Learning to Live What I Preach

Therefore everyone who hears these words of mine and puts them into practice is like a wise man who built his house on the rock. The rain came down, the streams rose, and the winds blew and beat against that house; yet it did not fall because it had its foundation on the rock (Matt. 7:24-25).

Not long after I'd spoken to the Methodist men's group, I was asked to speak at the First Baptist Church of Spindale men's fellowship dinner. This group was going to be much larger than my first engagement, creating an even greater struggle with my fear. But I was confident that God had opened the door, so I accepted their invitation, hoping that God would arrange my flight schedule so I'd have the day off. But it didn't work out the way I had expected. I was scheduled to be off the day of the dinner, but since I still only held a reserve pilot bid, I had to go on call at 5:00 a.m. the next morning; that meant I would have to respond to any quick call out in less than two hours, and I was still commuting over two hundred miles from my home to Atlanta. I figured God would work it out where there would be several pilots on call ahead of me. I knew that would give me ample time to get to Atlanta the next morning. However, I was wrong!

About two o'clock on the afternoon I was to speak, I called Eastern crew scheduling to find out what my position for call out would be when I went on duty the next morning, and my faith went right out the window when the scheduler told me, "You're our number one man to go."

My first impulse was to cancel the engagement. I knew they'd understand, but then I began to think about the prayer I'd prayed when God had first called me to witness for Him. I'd asked Him not to allow anyone to invite me to speak unless it was His will that I do so. I struggled with the decision right up to the last minute. Was I to catch a flight to Atlanta or speak to the Baptist men? That's when God asked me, "What do you plan to speak about to the men?"

"Putting our faith into action," I said.

"Then put your faith in action," He said. "Practice what you preach." And with a perfect sense of peace, I decided to keep the appointment. The dinner went well, and the men seemed to enjoy what I had to say, especially when I told them about how—after much anxiety—I'd exercised my trust in God by being there. In fact, many of them came up to me after the dinner to say what the evening had meant to them.

It was about 10:00 p.m. when I arrived home from the dinner, and I went to bed with a peaceful feeling, thinking I'd get up and catch the 7:30 a.m. flight out of Greenville-Spartanburg and be in position if the company needed me.

But the phone woke me at three o'clock in the morning. I sat straight up in the bed. I knew it had to be crew scheduling. *They probably need me for a five o'clock departure,* I thought. *Maybe I should lie and tell them I'm sick.* I switched on the light and turned to look at Charlotte.

"Maybe we shouldn't answer it," she said, knowing the struggle I'd gone through trying to make a decision about keeping the speaking engagement. Her sentiments echoed mine.

"At least I can claim I didn't get the call," I responded. But my conscience argued, "God will never honor a lie."

And, suddenly, with a newfound surge of faith, I looked at Charlotte, "We can't stop trusting God. Give me the phone."

"Hello," I stammered. It was Dan, one of my favorite schedulers. We'd often talked about the Lord together, and he knew about our work with the camp.

"Captain Fish," he said, "I need you for a 10:00 a.m. departure."

"Sure," I answered, letting out my breath. "That will be no problem at all." The 7:30 flight would get me there in plenty of time. I was so relieved I didn't even ask him where the flight would be taking me, even though I knew a sequence of flights could keep me out for as long as four days. *Maybe I can get some sleep now,* I thought.

But as soon as my head hit the pillow again, the Lord began speaking to me as clearly as I've ever heard Him: "You need to catch the 7:35 flight out of Charlotte—instead of Greenville-Spartanburg—so your truck will be there to get you back home. This flight you're going on will end up in Charlotte with a dead-head (ride in the passenger cabin) back to Atlanta. This way you can just drive home from Charlotte." I live an equal distance between the airports and normally fly out of Greenville-Spartanburg because it's in the direction of Atlanta which makes it easier if I have to drive all the way.

I sat straight up in bed again and told Charlotte what the Lord had just said to me. "Hand me the phone," I said. "I want to call Dan back." When he answered, I told him what had happened.

"Let me look, Captain Fish." he said amazed. "I don't remember where all it's going myself." The flight segments are computer generated from system control and sent to crew scheduling to assign flight crews. "Hmmmmm," he said, after a moment of silence. "It sure does end in Charlotte. You just deadhead from Atlanta to Tampa to replace a crew that's over limits on their hours, fly from Tampa to Miami, then to Charlotte where you'll finish and deadhead back to Atlanta."

After we'd hung up, I lay back for another few winks of sleep with Jesus' words from the Sermon on the Mount running through my mind. "Therefore whosoever heareth these sayings of mine, and doeth them, I will liken him unto a wise man, which built his house" (KJV).

After I'd gotten to Atlanta and started out on the flight, I discovered that not only would I finish in Charlotte, but I would have had to lay over there until the next day. Then I'd be free from duty for at least twelve hours after my scheduled return to Atlanta. In addition, I was going to receive a free day at home without having to worry about another call-out. With all the work needing to be done at the camp, God knew I could use a free day!

26

An Unforgettable Visit
of My In-laws

They replied, "Believe in the Lord Jesus Christ, and you will be saved—
you and your household" (Acts 16:31).

Paul and Silas were thrown into prison in Philippi for sharing
their faith. As they spent the night in jail singing praises to God,
an earthquake shook open the prison doors. The jailer was so
frightened by the earthquake and the thought that the men
would escape that he was about to take his own life. Paul called
out to him and told him that they were all there. Then in fear and
trembling, the jailer came to Paul and Silas and asked them the
universal question, "What must I do to be saved?" The interesting thing about Paul's answer was that he promised salvation to
the jailer "and thy house," meaning his whole family as well. I
believe that, with all of our hearts, we need to claim, through the
Spirit, the salvation of our families. Only the Spirit can deposit
those impulses in our hearts. To our families we owe our first
priority of witnessing. That's why I'll never forget the first
opportunity God gave Charlotte and me to witness to her mom
and dad, George and Selina Andersen.

It was winter, not long after Barbara's death, when Charlotte's
parents decided to leave the bitter cold of Buffalo and spend a
couple of weeks with us in our much milder climate. We were
glad they were coming, but we were worried about how they'd
react to our new life-style. Many people were turning to us by
that time, and we were openly ministering to them. Her parents
were good people, but they'd never shown much interest in
church. One of the things that had been bothering them was

what they considered our "flippant" way of accepting Barbara's death. Because they did not understand the gift of peace which God had given us, her dad had even accused us of not really loving her. Just before they arrived, Charlotte and I prayed together asking God not only to give us the boldness to continue carrying out our ministry while they were with us, but we asked God to confirm our work with signs and wonders so that her parents might also come to believe as we did.

No sooner had they arrived than the phone began to ring with people needing ministry. It didn't take long for Charlotte's mom to ask what was going on, and we were able to tell her about the way in which God had been using us. "In fact," Charlotte said, "I'm praying that God will send someone to our door now asking for ministry so that you might understand." Within minutes the doorbell rang. Charlotte answered the door as her mom looked on from the top of the steps of the foyer. A nervous young woman stood there.

"Are you Mrs. Fish?" the woman asked.

"Yes, I am. May I help you?" Charlotte replied.

"Well, someone told me I could talk to you. I really need help," the woman explained.

As Mrs. Andersen watched, Charlotte invited the woman in and proceeded to minister to her and pray with her. This was only the beginning of the unusual ways in which God worked to help Charlotte's mom and dad to believe. Almost every day of their visit, a new confirming sign took place. Mr. Andersen began reading some of the testimonial books in our collection. One evening we had a big laugh around the supper table when he said, "O. A., I've finally figured out how to get saved."

"How's that?" I asked.

"Well, first of all, I have to be an alcoholic, a drug addict, or some sort of despicable character; at least, that's how all those people I've been reading about seemed to make it." Then he asked, "Isn't there some way a decent, good person can be saved without having to go through all that?" We all laughed, but it was obvious that his hunger for God was growing.

Our evening meals together seemed to be the time when God brought things out to be discussed. At another time we were hurrying to finish eating so that I would be ready to commute to Atlanta. I didn't really want to go. "Lord," I silently prayed during the meal. "It would be great if I could get a flight that originates in Charlotte in the morning so I wouldn't have to go to Atlanta."

That inward voice of the Spirit which I'd come to recognize said, "Why don't you ask aloud for Me to do this?"

"But, Lord," I said, "I don't want to put You on the spot. And I don't want to cause Grandpa's faith to falter in case it's not Your will to do this."

"Are you worried about him or saving your face?" He asked.

It was embarrassing to admit, but I knew that was the real reason. After an inward struggle, I muttered under my breath, half hoping no one would pay any attention. "You know what?" I asked. And no one did pay any attention—except Grandpa.

"No, what?" he asked.

"Oh, ah, I was just sitting here silently praying, and I asked my Heavenly Father, if it was pleasing to Him, to give me a flight that starts in Charlotte instead of having to go to Atlanta tonight."

"Does that happen often?" he asked smiling.

"What? My praying?" I asked.

"No," he laughed, "getting a flight that starts out in Charlotte."

"Not before," I said.

No calls came from crew scheduling, so I grudgingly picked up my suitcase and drove to Charlotte to catch my planned commuter flight. When I checked in with flight operations to get the jump seat (an observer seat located in the cockpit), I overheard a New York-based captain talking on the company telephone. He was saying to his crew scheduler that he would not have the minimum required rest time for his early morning departure out of Charlotte. When he hung up, I asked what he flew. "The DC 9," he said. This was the same as me. I knew there was no way for the New York scheduler to get the flight covered and out on time with a New York crew. So I called Atlanta crew scheduling and offered to cover the flight. But the scheduler said that unless the company specifically requested him to do so, he couldn't authorize the covering of the New York base's flying.

"Well," I sighed, "if you decide you want me to do it, call me before my flight leaves for Atlanta in ten minutes."

So I went to the departure gate and waited. The minutes passed, and no call came. Finally, I asked the Lord. "What does all this mean? You—at least, I thought it was You—prompted me to speak my request aloud at the supper table. Then nothing happened before I left home, and now it couldn't have been a coincidence that I overheard the New York captain's conversation."

Disappointed, I boarded my flight at the last second. We had already started the engines and began turning out from the gate when the gate agent came running, waving for us to stop. I picked up my bag and headed for the door. It was a relief to know that God hadn't let me down. "Captain Fish," the agent said.

"Yes," I interrupted, stopping him in mid-sentence. "I know what it's all about."

I got off the plane and made my way first to the telephone to let Grandpa Andersen know. He said, "That's amazing! That's amazing!"

I found a motel in Charlotte and went to bed still wondering why God had let the drama go so far before answering my prayer. After all that had happened, it would have been easier probably for me to have gone on to Atlanta. But as I recalled the astonishment in Grandpa's voice, I realized that God had answered my prayer for Grandpa Andersen's sake, not mine, in order to strengthen his faith. It had nothing to do with me and my selfish reasons for wanting it to happen. It was procrastination, laziness, and self-interest that caused me to ask—not really caring about the commitment I owed to my flying career—another lesson I've tried hard not to forget.

The most intensive working of God during my in-laws' visit came near the end of their stay. Charlotte's sister Joan and her husband, who lived in Buffalo, were having marriage trouble. Joan who was depressed had been calling Charlotte in the middle of the night to talk. She didn't want their parents to know, but after a few nights, Charlotte was finally able to convince Joan to let her tell their mom and dad what was going on. So on the afternoon before they were to leave to go home, Charlotte told them. Mrs. Andersen called Joan on the telephone right away, but when she found out how depressed Joan was and that she wasn't being helped, she gave the phone to me. "Here, O. A., you talk to her," she said.

I took the phone, but I could tell right away that Joan wasn't hearing a thing I was saying. So I asked, "Joan, may I pray with you?"

"Yes, pray with her," Mrs. Andersen urged.

As I began to pray, Charlotte left the sink where she'd been preparing supper and came over to take my hand to offer agreement in prayer: " 'If two of you shall agree on earth as touching any thing that they shall ask, it shall be done for them of my Father which is in heaven' (Matt. 18:19, KJV). Lord, please send someone to Joan who can minister to her in person. Right now, she needs your help. In Jesus' name, Amen."

After we hung up and sat down to eat supper, Mrs. Andersen was still so worried; she couldn't eat. Finally she said, "If I just knew someone in Buffalo who I could call and get them to go check on her."

"Grandma," I said gently, "didn't you hear what I prayed for when I was on the phone with Joan?"

"Yes," she said. "You asked God to send someone to her."

"That's right. Now go ahead and eat. God is answering our prayer," I said.

Grandma seemed to be satisfied for the moment. However, that night after Grandpa had gone to bed, she talked Charlotte into going with her to the basement, bedroom telephone so she could call Joan back. Later, when Charlotte came to bed, she told me what had happened.

When Joan answered the phone, she was a totally new person. She said a pastor whom she really liked from the church up the street had unexpectedly dropped by. And while he was at the house ministering to Joan, her husband had called. She'd asked the pastor if he'd be willing to talk with her husband. He'd agreed, and at that moment, they were at the church talking.

Mrs. Andersen had been so overwhelmed at the dramatic way God was answering our prayer that she'd just handed the phone to Charlotte and without saying a word, slumped back on the bed. Charlotte began saying to her sister, "Talk to God. Tell Him how you feel. You'll be surprised to find that you'll come to love Him. He knows how you feel, and He wants to help you." At the same time, her mom picked up Oral Roberts's book *Three Most Important Steps to Your Better Health and Miracles* that was lying next to the bed and flipped it open to page 136. She began to read, "Talk to God. Tell Him how you feel. You may be surprised. He knows how you feel and wants to help you." Almost the exact words that Charlotte, who was on the other side of the bed, was speaking to Joan. Cold chills raced over me the whole time Charlotte was telling me the story.

Early the next morning, I had breakfast with Mr. and Mrs. Andersen. My flight to Atlanta was leaving the Charlotte airport at about the same time as their flight for Buffalo. So they were going to ride in with me. We were sitting there eating quietly when Mr. Andersen looked over at his wife, "You know, Babe, if I stay in this house one more day, I'm really going to be a believer."

"I know," she said. Then she brought out the book she'd been holding behind her. I knew what was coming, but I sat quietly as she told us the story Charlotte had related to me the night before. It was the first time I'd seen Mrs. Andersen's eyes filled with tears. Mr. Andersen sat in stunned silence.

Later, during our hour-plus drive to the Charlotte Airport, Mr. Andersen said, "O. A., only eternity will tell how much our visit with you two has meant to me." This gave even more meaning to the why of Barbara's death since she'd really loved her Grandma and Grandpa Andersen so much, and nothing could have pleased her more than knowing that they'd come to know her Lord Jesus.

It was only a short time after that visit that we received a call early one morning that Mr. Andersen, too, had gone to meet our Lord and his. He had died suddenly of a heart attack.

27
Witnessing on the Airline

Ye are the light of the world. . . . Let your light so shine before men, that they may see your good works, and glorify your Father which is in heaven (Matt. 5:14-16, KJV).

As time went on, I noticed a remarkable increase in opportunities to share my faith at work. Everywhere I looked, people were hungry to talk about God.

* * * * *

One day, I was flying a one-day turnaround from Atlanta to Miami and back. My copilot was Al Moore, a nice-looking, congenial, young man in his early forties. It was the first time I'd flown with Al. We were on our way back into Atlanta, and Al was doing the flying while I worked the radios. Just before the approach for some reason, the Lord impressed upon me to tell Al about the tremendous peace He'd given Charlotte and me concerning Barbara's death. And as I talked, I noticed tears in Al's eyes. "I didn't mean to upset you," I apologized.

"Oh, what you are saying didn't upset me. I guess, it's just that what you've said has made me feel so ashamed. Here, you and your wife have just lost a daughter, and you're praising the Lord. My wife and I are going to have a baby, and we're mad at the world—and God," he said.

"Why are you angry?" I asked.

"Well, we've both just turned forty, and our other children are already in their teens. We just feel like God has tricked us," he admitted. After a moment's hesitation, Al continued, "I don't know what it is that you have, O. A., but whatever it is, it's something I'd like to have."

"Maybe we can talk when we get on the ground," I said. After we'd landed, I told him about how God had filled me with His Holy Spirit. I suggested some Scriptures for him to study and books to read on the subject. A few weeks later, I ran into Al again. He was beaming from ear to ear.

"O. A.," he said, "you're now talking to a Spirit-filled Christian. My wife and I both are Christians, and we can't wait for our baby to get here."

"That's great," I shouted as I gave him a big hug. About two years later I saw Al, proudly showing off his beautiful little daughter in the pilot's crew lounge.

* * * * *

An unusual testimony for our Lord began one day when I checked in at the flight operations desk. "It's going to be a good flight," I said to Bruce Smith, my copilot and long-time friend. Bruce was a true Christian and a pleasure to fly with. Then I added, "No, it's going to be a *great* flight." I had just glanced at my crew list and saw who our senior flight attendant was going to be: Barbara Armstrong, another Spirit-filled Christian friend. In fact, Barbara had spent a week at our camp on two occasions, along with several other flight attendants and pilots. They had helped us build all the cabins in our girls' campsite.

We were to fly from Atlanta to Nashville for the first leg of our flight. It was a hot summer day, and every seat of the DC 9-31 was filled. Everything was routine except for a longer than normal takeoff roll due to the hot weather and our heavy load. But just at rotation, we heard an explosion and smelled burning rubber. Our outside tire on the left main gear had blown. The flying rubber had taken out the gear-warning switch, a chunk from our flaps, and some pieces had gone into our left engine intake. "Well, I thought it was going to be a good flight," I quipped, looking over at Bruce's nervous smile. He picked up his mike and advised the tower of what was happening and told them we would remain in the local area to assess our situation.

In the air we discovered that we had no left-gear warning

light. That meant we had no way of being certain that the gear was down and locked. In spite of ingesting some rubber, the left engine appeared to be running normally. But we didn't know the extent of flap damage or whether the other tire on that gear was intact.

I called Barbara to the front and advised her of the situation. "We've blown a tire, or, at least, we think it's just one, and we'll be flying around in the area for a while to assess our damage and our options. Would you please tell the people I'll talk to them as soon as I can."

When Barbara started to make her announcement, I switched on my monitor so I could listen to what she said. "Ladies and gentlemen," she began with a strong deliberate voice, "Captain Fish has just advised me that we've blown a tire, and we'll have to fly around for a while to assess the damage." Then very hurriedly, she added, "but you don't have to worry about a thing. Your whole crew is Christian." Now, I admit Barbara was rather gushy. Christians do die in plane crashes, on the highways, and a thousand other places, but I think Barbara was doing her best to console the passengers. I could hear the applause all the way up to the cockpit.

After consulting with our experts on the ground, I made a low, slow pass over the runway while our maintenance crew observed the damage through binoculars. They told me that the gear looked to be down and locked and that the other tire appeared to be OK. They also told me about the chunk missing from the trailing edge flaps.

After climbing back up to altitude, I lowered the flaps to the landing position and found that the damage had minimal effect on the flight characteristics. The only thing left to do was fly around for a couple of hours and burn up fuel, to lighten our load as much as possible, and pray that the other tire held up on landing.

Everything went smoothly. There was no problem with the landing, and after another hour's delay on the ground, we boarded another airplane. Soon we were on our way to Nashville. It all resulted in some complimentary letters and a good ending some time later. While coming out of Knoxville one Sunday afternoon, a commuting flight attendant came up to the cockpit to introduce herself. When she saw me, she became excited, "Captain Fish!" she said, "Do you remember me?"

"No," I had to confess.

"I was the extra flight attendant on your flight when we blew the tire coming out of Atlanta."

"Oh, yes, I remember now," I said.

"And do you remember Barbara telling the passengers that we were all Christians?" she asked.

"How could I forget?" I laughed.

"Well, I wasn't," she said, and then broke out in a wide grin, "but praise the Lord, I am now. I was baptized this morning."

* * * * *

Another memorable opportunity God gave me to witness was with co-pilot Bob Shaw. The first time I met Bob, we were teamed together on a three-day flight. He was a tall, outgoing fellow. However, the first couple days of our flying together, he said very little. *Maybe he knows about my Christian walk and doesn't know how to approach it,* I thought. But one of the things I'd always tried to do while on duty was to avoid controversial subjects that could distract our attention from the safe and effective operation of the flight. So I never introduced the subject of religion or politics, but if another person brought up God, then I was always ready to talk.

Bob and I were on the last leg of our three-day sequence, a nonstop, night flight from New York to Atlanta. The night was clear and the stars bright. Sitting there in the darkened cockpit with nothing but the soft glow of the instrument panel lighting was like being a part of that vast universe outside our window. My thoughts turned to Bob sitting quietly on my right. *Lord,* I said, *Bob seems like a nice guy, but somehow I just don't feel he knows You in a personal way. I've been with him for three days, and I haven't had an opportunity to share You with him. I wish You'd give me that opportunity.*

It was as though Bob had been reading my mind. "You know what," he said. "I believe in God, but I don't believe in a personal intervening God."

"Bob," I exclaimed. "I wish you hadn't waited until this last leg to say that."

"Why not?" he asked.

"Because, I'd like to have the chance to show you a personal intervening God," I told him.

"Oh, yeah?" he said halfheartedly.

"Oh, yeah!" I said. "And I'm believing God will let me fly with you again soon, so I can show you that He's exactly that."

"That'll be interesting," he said.

That would be interesting, I thought, because I was still flying reserve and seldom flew with the same copilot during a short span of time. There were over a hundred DC-9 copilots based in Atlanta then, and the chances were slim that Bob and I would have a chance to fly together again soon.

But a few weeks later, that personal intervention Bob had doubted began with a series of incredible events, and the only logical explanation was that they were planned by God.

It began one morning when I had to make a quick trip to the plumber's house to pick up a part. Our plumber, Bill Brock, and his wife Blanche are close Christian friends of ours. At the time, their son-in-law, Sam Whaley, had just gone into ministry and was working with Kenneth Hagan, another well-known minister. The two were conducting meetings across the country. After getting to the part I wanted, I was standing there talking to Blanche when the mail carrier came. "Oh," Blanche said, "here's a letter from Sam and Jane." Knowing that I was interested in what was happening in their lives, she opened it right away. "Guess what," she said as she read along, "They're going to be in Saint Louis in a couple of days." My ears perked up. I was going to be in Saint Louis in a couple of days myself. I had been assigned an evening flight that was subject to a layover in Saint Louis on the same day Sam and Jane were going to be there. "It says here that they'll be at the Stagton Ballroom in Saint Louis Thursday morning."

"That's wonderful! I'm going to be in Saint Louis on that day, too. I told Sam that someday God would work it out so I could attend one of their meetings on a layover," I told Blanche. I was excited as I hurried back home to get ready to leave on my trip.

Charlotte was as excited as I was. We stood at the door chatting just before I left. But I noticed that she kept looking at my **uniform sleeves. She said "You know, Honey, the stripes on this jacket** are really beginning to fray. You need to get a new uniform."

"I know. I ordered one, but when I went to pick it up in Atlanta, the shop had gone out of business. Now I'll have to go to another shop, and that'll take at least six weeks, but praise God. He will provide," I replied.

A trip to the plumber had caused me to run a little late, so I hurriedly jumped into my pickup and headed for the Greenville-Spartanburg Jetport to catch my commuter flight. It had been raining all morning, but the rain finally stopped about the time I drove past Spartanburg on Interstate 85. That's when I noticed the rear of the truck wavering a bit. "Must have a tire going flat," I muttered as I pulled over and stopped, looking down at my watch. I barely had ten minutes to spare before missing my flight. "Lord," I said, "I'm sure going to need Your help if I'm going to get this tire changed in less than ten minutes."

I grabbed my jack and lug wrench from behind the seat and jumped out. I had the wheel jacked up in seconds, but when I tried to loosen the lugs, I discovered the single socket lug I had wouldn't fit. I dropped the wrench to the ground and raised both hands toward heaven. "You've really got a problem now," I said.

Then I heard a screech and looked up to see a car braking to a halt. It took three- or four-hundred feet for the driver to get stopped, and he spun his wheels backing up to where I was. "Buddy, it looks like you've got a problem," he said as he got out and hurried back to where I was standing.

"Sure do. I've got a flat, and my lug wrench is the wrong size," I told him.

"Well, it just so happens I threw a four-pronged lug wrench in my truck this morning," he said as he went to retrieve it. "Wondered why I did that."

My spare tire was mounted up under the back of my truck and was splattered with rain and mud. "Here," the man said, "you take the flat off, and I'll get your spare out so you won't get all dirty." Together we quickly got the tire on, and he tightened the lugs while I reached down to get the flat tire to throw it into the truck. As I did so, I noticed his crippled left hand. It had been severed some time in the past, leaving him with only his thumb and about half of his index finger. It was amazing how aptly he was using it. The scripture from Hebrews 13 came to mind that speaks of entertaining angels unaware.

"Hmmmm," I thought, as he jumped back into his car and sped away with hardly time for me to say, "Thanks!" Then suddenly realizing how short my own time was, I glanced down at my watch while getting back into my truck. The dramatic event had used up exactly ten minutes.

I reached the airport just in time to run up the loading stairs as the agent was preparing to close the door on my flight. The flight attendant motioned for me to sit in an empty seat on the front row of the first-class cabin next to a lady who appeared to be very nervous.

"Are you a pilot?" she asked as I fastened my seat belt.

"Yes, I am. I've been flying for Eastern for twenty years."

"God must have sent you to sit by me," she said. "Normally I'm not nervous at all about flying. But it was so foggy driving over from my home in the mountains in Franklin that by the time I got here, my nerves were shot."

"It's going to be OK," I said, patting her hand. Soon we were lost in conversation. We talked about her home and family. We discussed her restaurant, the Sunrise Cafe, and a lot about God. She forgot about being nervous, and before either of us knew it, we were landing in Atlanta.

I knew I had about two hours before my flight was scheduled to depart Atlanta and remembered Charlotte's comments earlier, so I decided to visit a uniform shop I'd heard was located near the airport. A friendly, older man met me as I walked in the door. He took one look at my worn jacket and knew why I was there. "What size do you wear?" He asked.

"You'll have to measure me for a fit," I told him. "I have rounded shoulders, and it's hard to fit me off the rack." He left and came back in a minute with an Eastern pilot's jacket.

"Here, try this on," he said. It was a perfect fit. "Hmmmm,

that's interesting," he mumbled and left to get the matching pants. They too were a perfect fit. "Would you believe that the captain who ordered this uniform just called this morning and said he wouldn't be picking it up. He'd just learned he'd been grounded for a heart condition. It's yours if you want it."

After all that had happened on this day, I was speechless. "But I don't have enough money with me," I stammered. "Not even a check. Can you take a credit card?"

"Don't worry," He laughed. Then he handed me a business card with the price written on the back and said, "Just mail me a check when you get a chance." So I walked out of his shop wearing a shiny new uniform.

I got back to the airport and flight operations in plenty of time to check out my flight plan. I signed the dispatch release and then headed for my airplane. I hadn't bothered checking to see who my copilot would be. I knew whoever it was, he would be out doing his job of preflighting the aircraft, but when I looked in the cockpit door, there was Bob Shaw, the pilot who didn't believe in an intervening God. The first words out of his mouth were, "Hi, O. A. What's God done for you lately?"

"Let me just tell you what He's done so far today," I laughed as I climbed into my seat.

As I brought him up to date, I watched his sly smile change to a serious expression. Occasionally, he'd interject, "That's amazing! That's incredible! That's unbelievable!"

I had a sudden inspiration: "You think what I've been telling you is incredible. Then let me tell you about something God's going to do—before He does it."

"Shoot," he said. "Let me hear it."

"Well, I have this friend in the ministry who's going to be in Saint Louis while we're there. All I know is he's supposed to be speaking at the Stagton Ballroom. I have no idea at all where that is, but I want you to pay attention to how God will work it out for me to meet up with my friend."

"OK," Bob laughed. "You and God have my undivided attention."

It was late evening when we arrived in Saint Louis to begin our layover. We were standing at the courtesy car pickup point when

I noticed a long, black-and-white zebra-striped limousine drive up. Mounted on the top of the limousine was what looked like the bow of a boat with animal heads hanging out in every direction. "What in the world is that?" I asked.

Bob and our two flight attendants laughed. "That's our ride," Bob said. "Didn't you know? We now stay at a place called Noah's Ark." I got kind of worried then. I had no idea where this new layover hotel was located. The last place where I had laid over was near downtown Saint Louis, and that's where I supposed the Stagton Ballroom would be. I didn't say anything, but when we came out of the airport road and the driver turned in the opposite direction—away from Saint Louis—I began to get even more anxious.

"Now Lord," I said, "I've told Bob You were going to put me in touch with Sam, and Sam is supposed to be back that way. What's this going to do to Bob when You don't deliver on what was promised." I tried not to squirm around in the seat too much. I knew Bob was watching my reaction and probably enjoying my discomfort. Finally, I asked the driver where this Noah's Ark was located.

"In Saint Charles," he said.

"How far is that from Saint Louis?" I gulped.

"About twenty miles," he said.

My heart sank. *This is it,* I thought. *I've made a fool out of myself and discredited God.* But the longer I sat there, the more I had to admit that I was more worried about looking foolish myself than discrediting God. So finally I asked the Lord to forgive me of my pridefulness and to do whatever was necessary to help Bob believe—no matter how it made me look.

It was after 11:00 p.m. when we arrived at the hotel and began checking in. The lobby was empty except for my crew. After we'd all finished, I lingered behind as the rest of them headed for the elevator. "Do you happen to know where the Stagton Ballroom is located in Saint Louis?" I asked the check-in clerk.

"I've never heard of a Stagton Ballroom in Saint Louis," he said.

"You haven't?" I asked.

"No, not in Saint Louis, but there is a Stagton Ballroom just on the other side of our parking lot." Fireworks went off in my head. I couldn't wait to tell Bob. He and the flight attendants were waiting for me at the elevator.

As I stepped inside, and the door shut, Bob was standing right next to me with the flight attendants behind us. "Bob," I said quietly, "Do you know where the Stagton Ballroom is?"

"No," he answered also speaking in a hushed voice.

"Just across the parking lot!" I said nodding in the direction where the clerk had pointed.

Bob fell down on his knees and started pounding on the elevator wall. I couldn't help laughing as the flight attendants yelled, "What in the world is wrong with you?"

"I'm not going to tell you," he said shaking his head. "Besides, you wouldn't believe me if I did."

A quick telephone call the next morning confirmed that the Stagton Ballroom next door was indeed the place where Sam would be speaking. The meeting was to begin at 10:00 a.m., so I arrived at the auditorium about 9:00. Sam and Jane were there getting things set up. He gave me a big hug and kept saying, "You said you were going to surprise us some day, and you're here!"

After the morning was over, we decided to go for lunch. As we were driving out of the parking lot, I saw Bob jogging. I had Sam pull over long enough to introduce them. From that day on, whenever I flew with Bob or ran into him anywhere on the system, he was hungry to hear what God was doing in my life. In fact it became a standard greeting between us. "O. A.," he'd yell. "What's God done for you lately?"

I'd yell back, "You wouldn't believe me if I told you."

Then we'd both say, "Try me," and laugh.

28
A Unique Invitation to Appear on the "700 Club"

Humble yourself in the sight of the Lord, and he shall lift you up (Jas. 4:10, KJV).

Once I had yielded myself to the Lord to be a witness, He opened the doors of opportunity, putting me to work. Almost monthly, I found myself speaking to churches, schools, clubs, Christian men's groups, and even some radio appearances. Except for those monthly engagements, most of my days off from the airline were spent working at our camp. There were always many things to be done. I hired Ralph Nichols, a good, all-around handyman to work for the camp.

Ralph was the president of the local chapter of the Full Gospel Businessmen's Fellowship International, and that year, they were holding their annual regional convention in nearby Asheville. Ralph felt he should go as chapter president, but we had so much work to do I just didn't see how we could work it out. But during my prayer time the night before the convention, the Lord clearly spoke to me, "Go to the convention. There will be someone there that you need to meet." After sharing my impressions from the Lord with Charlotte and Ralph, we all decided to go.

It was a good convention, but as the days went by, I still hadn't figured out why God had insisted that I go. I was beginning to wonder if maybe I'd just imagined I'd heard God. But one day after lunch, I was standing next to an entrance door of the hotel where we were meeting when the door swung open, almost knocking me over. And bounding through the door came Ben Kinchlow, popular cohost of the "700 Club," who was one of the speakers at the convention. He apologized for almost hitting me and mumbled something about having to hurry to the airport as he disappeared from the building.

As I watched Kinchlow hurry away, the Lord again spoke to my spirit, "That's the man you are here to meet."

Now I'm really confused, I thought. *If this is the man I'm to meet, why's he hurrying off to catch a plane? It doesn't make any sense at all.* Charlotte and Ralph were standing in the hotel lobby. When I told them what had happened, they both just smiled and shrugged.

"Hon," Charlotte said, "I'm afraid you're going to have to work through this one on your own. I can't help you."

So I excused myself and retreated into a meeting hall where the youth were having a session. A dynamic speaker was conducting the meeting, and except for his speaking, the place was totally quiet. It was a good place to get alone with my thoughts and try to sort things out. I sat down in a chair off to the side of the auditorium and leaned back against the wall. Soon I was lost in a one-way conversation with God: "If Ben was the man I was supposed to meet, why wait until he left to tell me?"

Suddenly my thoughts were scattered by a phone ringing. It was mounted on the wall right above my head, and the ringing was distracting the meeting so I reached up and pulled the receiver off the hook. I didn't really intend to answer it—just silence it—assuming someone had the wrong number, but I heard someone yelling into the receiver, "Hello, Hello!"

So I pulled the receiver to my ear and said, "Hello. Who are you calling?"

"This is Ben Kinchlow," the voice said. "I'm at the airport, and I've just discovered my Bible is missing. I think I left it in that room at the podium. Can you check on it for me?"

At first I was too stunned to speak. Then finally I said, "Yes, yes, hold on, and I'll get an usher to check on it."

By this time an usher had walked over to where I was sitting, and I told him about the situation. He went to check the podium, so I said, "Hello, Ben, I have someone looking for it now."

"Thanks," he said, and then to kill time he asked, "By the way, who am I speaking to?"

"Captain Fish," I said.

"Captain? What sort of Captain are you?" he asked.

"An airline captain," I said, and then I went on to tell him who I flew for.

"Brother, I don't believe we've had an airline captain on the '700 Club.' How about sending me a resume? I'd like to recommend you as a guest on the program," Ben told me. There was no way I'd have had the nerve to accept such an invitation except for the fact that God had shown me so dramatically this was His doing, and it was His will for me to do it.

By then the usher was back with Ben's Bible, and I assured him I would see that it was forwarded to him. "And don't forget," he said again before hanging up, "to send me your resume."

Charlotte and Ralph were just as awed as I was when I told them what had taken place. As soon as I was home, I put a resume in the mail. Then a few weeks later, I received a telegram asking me to call Jackie Mitchum, guest coordinator for the "700 Club." When I called her, she said "Hello, Captain Fish, this is Jackie Mitchum. Remember me?"

I was stunned. How was I supposed to know her? Not wanting to sound dumb, I said, "I'm afraid you're going to have to refresh my memory."

She said, "I used to be George Otis's secretary, and I met you and your family on our tour to Israel a few years ago." My family and I had gone on Mr. Otis's High Adventure tour in 1977 along with over a thousand other guests. We had met Jackie in the Ben Gurion Airline terminal in Tel Aviv for one brief moment.

I remembered then, but how did she remember us after such a brief encounter, I wondered. "Yes, I do remember you now," I said.

"Captain Fish," she continued, "You'll never guess what happened. Ben gave me your resume, and as soon as I read it, I remembered meeting you. While I was looking it over Pat Robertson walked up to my desk and said, 'Jackie, do we know of an airline pilot that we could use in an endorsement for our upcoming telethon?' I told him I was holding your letter in my hand, so he asked that I get in touch with you. Will you do it for us?" she asked. Then she went on to explain that they wanted to have a camera crew and producer meet me at the Atlanta's Hartsfield Airport to shoot some footage of me going through my flight preparation routine, and then I was to do an endorsement for the "700 Club" while being videotaped in the cockpit. The palms of my hands were sweating from fear at the mere thought of doing it, but God's fingerprints were so vividly present in all that was happening that I couldn't say no.

The dreaded day finally arrived, and I found myself pretending to be filling out flight papers in operations with a television camera in my face and a roomful of pilots ribbing me. The camera crew then shot some footage of me strolling down the concourse, talking to passengers on the plane, and, finally, we did the endorsement spot while I was seated in the cockpit. An hour or more of shooting would be edited to seconds and aired several times throughout that year's "700 Club" telethon. *I sure am glad that's over,* I thought, not realizing that God had further plans for me in television. The endorsement spot was just the introduction.

A few months later I was asked to do a guest appearance on the "700 Club" program. One day, I was walking across the parking apron of the old Atlanta terminal to my airplane, thinking about the upcoming appearance on TV and how almost boring my airline career had been. "God, You've blessed my years of flying so wonderfully, that it's hard to think of any exciting stories to tell if I'm asked."

When I got to the departure gate, I soon forgot about what I was going to say on the "700 Club" and lost myself in preparing for my flight up to Greensboro. The passenger boarding was completed, everything checked out, and soon we were roaring down the runway toward another one of my "routine" flights. "Gear up," I snapped to the copilot as soon as we were safely airborne, but that's where the routine bit ended.

Suddenly, it felt like the nose of the airplane was mounted on top of a jackhammer. We were shaking so hard that the instruments were unreadable. I had a good idea of what had gone wrong. Somehow, the whirling nose tires had jammed with the wheelwell doors. "Gear down," I yelled to the copilot. He put the handle down, but nothing seemed to happen. The two main gear "down and safe" greens indicated normal, but there was no green light for the nose gear. By this time the tire rotation had halted, and the shaking subsided. However, we were left with a nose wheel jammed somewhere in the mid-retracted position.

As I began to plan what lay ahead, there was a little echo somewhere in the back of my mind: "You wanted a testimony to share; well, it's in the making." If the situation hadn't been so serious, it would have been humorous. "Lord," I vowed. "Help me not to complain about Your blessings again."

After the control tower had been notified of our problem, I turned the flying chores over to the copilot. Within minutes I had all the skilled expertise our company could offer on the radio lending their assistance. I briefed the flight attendants and passengers of our problem and arranged to do a low altitude fly-by over the runway to give maintenance a chance to survey the problem. They only confirmed what we already knew. "Yep, Captain," the maintenance foreman said, "she's sure stuck all right." He couldn't tell whether or not the tires were blown.

We then climbed back up to altitude and cycled the gear handle up and down while we performed, within safe limits, every maneuver in the book that we thought might help to unstick the jammed gear: steep turns, pull-ups, slow flight, and various combinations, but nothing worked. Together we finally decided that maybe it might become unstuck if I bumped the main gear down pretty hard on landing. So the flight attendants prepared the cabin and readied the passengers for a possible rough landing. We were on final approach and down to about five-hundred feet when I prayed, "Lord, we've done all we know to do. Now I'm committing our lives into Your hands." Just then the copilot suggested trying cycling the gear handle one more time. This time as soon as he moved the handle back down, I heard a familiar sssssh as the gear slid down and locked, and my eyes fastened on three, beautiful green lights.

"Thank you, Lord," I said as we touched down smoothly and began a normal rollout. The tires had not blown in spite of the abuse they'd received from the wheel well doors. Later, as we continued on to Greenville with another plane, I informed the passengers about all that had happened, including the last-minute prayer. A loud cheer went up in the cabin, and one passenger wrote to Eastern thanking management for hiring Christian pilots.

Sure enough, I did get to tell this experience on the "700 Club." God used my appearance on the "700 Club" as another stepping-stone. Jimmy Thompson, president of WGGS-TV in Greenville, South Carolina, saw the program live on his station, and he invited me to appear on their syndicated Christian talk show called Nite Line. I soon became a frequent guest on the program, then a fill-in cohost, and eventually, a fill-in host.

29

My Introduction to George Otis and the Middle East

Awake, awake, O Zion,
clothe yourself with strength.
Put on your garments of splendor,
O Jerusalem, the holy city (Isa. 52:1).

Besides our work with the Hopewell Hoodlums and building the camp, Charlotte and I found ourselves involved in another ministry: our own Monday night Bible study. We had been leaning toward the idea of starting one when God sent us Sue Harding, a spiritually hungry neighbor, who wanted us to have one. We were soon joined by some other faithful ladies: Eularied Bradley, Carolyn Curtis, Mary Murray, Juanita Randall, and Winnie Smart. Others came and went, but these ladies couldn't seem to get enough of God's Word. Our first three years of study was on the Book of Revelation. Our studies led us to see that we truly are on the cutting edge of time, and God has prepared Israel and the Middle East as a stage upon which the last acts of prophecy are to be fulfilled. We spent much time studying maps of the Holy Land, and we dreamed of someday traveling there, especially Charlotte and I.

Harry Tysinger, an Eastern copilot, told me about George Otis. Harry had recently returned from one of George's High Adventure Holy Land Tours. What appealed to me about the tours was that Charlotte and I could save money by utilizing my interline pass privilege in El Al Airlines. Harry gave me a book, *High Adventure,* the autobiography of George Otis. From George's book, I learned that he, too, had come from an aviation background, having risen through the corporate ranks to become general manager for the Lear Jet Corporation. I also learned how God has used him as an instrument in leading Pat and Shirley Boone to the fullness of the Spirit. In fact, another appealing thing about George's next Holy Land tour was that Pat planned to go, so it didn't take a lot of selling to convince Charlotte and our daughters—Cheryl, Lisa, and Kim—about going on that tour in 1977. The tour was so heavily booked that our family had to travel to Israel two days early to be able to use our "space available" passes on El Al, but the money we would save on airfares was worth it.

Our flight on an El Al Boeing 747 jumbo jet was gorgeous, just eleven and one-half hours with a stop in London. The memorable thing about the flight was just before descent into the David Ben-Gurion Airport in Tel Aviv. The Israeli national anthem began playing over the public address system. The jubilant Jewish people, stirred by a passion for their homeland, were laughing, crying, singing, and dancing in the aisles. It was so moving that my family still talks about it today.

It was just past midnight, New York time, when our flight began, but because we passed through six time zones, the early winter sun was already setting the next day when we landed at the Ben-Gurion Airport. After dragging our large suitcases from the conveyer belt in baggage claim, my brain was so fatigued from jet lag that I could hardly think. I found myself standing in the middle of a mountain of bags with Charlotte and the girls all huddled around saying, "Daddy, what are we going to do now?"

Because of the uncertainty of getting on any particular flight, I had elected not to make hotel reservations in advance. Besides the El Al travel agent who gave me our passes assured me there would be no problem getting rooms. What I had not counted on, however, was arriving in Tel Aviv too tired to think. We were startled by a sharp male voice with a heavy Jewish accent that came from out of nowhere, "What are you people doing here?" We turned to see a large stocky gentleman lumbering toward us. "Are you with High Adventure?" he sounded somewhat irritated.

"Well, yes, but . . . " I said.

"Do you have a hotel?" he asked.

"No," I said. "We came early because . . ."

"I know!" he interrupted. "I just happened to be passing the window and saw your High Adventure baggage tags. Wait here," he demanded, "and I'll be right back." Within minutes, he was back, grabbing a couple of the girls' larger bags, he nodded, "Follow me." We hurriedly dragged the rest of our luggage toward an Israeli customs agent. Our rescuing stranger snapped, "It's OK, they're with me." With a broad grin the agent waved us through. When we reached the curb, this stranger hustled us over to a waiting cab, talked to the driver for a few minutes in Hebrew, and then turned to me as we threw our bags into the trunk. He said, "The driver will take you to the Diplomat Hotel in Jerusalem; you're not to pay him anything, not even a tip."

"But you don't understand," I again tried to explain. "These two days were supposed to be at our own expense." But the gentleman just wouldn't listen.

"Don't worry. It's OK," he said and shooed us into the taxicab.

The 35-mile-night drive to Jerusalem was horrifying. Of all my rides in New York cabs, none was like that one. Our hearts were in our mouths the whole time as we raced along the two-lane, blacktopped road, passing car after car on blind curves and against oncoming headlights that appeared to be right in our face. Charlotte ducked behind the front seat and wailed, "It would be a shame to make it this far and then be killed in a cab."

However, we did arrive safely. An army of smiling bellhops met us in front of the large, granite-constructed Diplomat Hotel. (I'm sure our three good-looking daughters had something to do with those smiles.) They escorted us and our bags through the lobby to seats near the check-in desk. The cab driver went over to the clerk and began chatting away with him in Hebrew. Every once in a while the clerk would look over at us, smile, and nod his head. In a few moments he motioned for us to come over and register.

When I tried to tip our driver, he strongly refused it. He wished us a good stay and left. I turned to the clerk and tried to explain to him that we were supposed to pay our own expenses for the next two days until our tour began. He smiled as though he didn't understand a word I was saying and nodded, "It's OK. Everything's OK."

The spacious rooms he assigned us were lovely. One look and Charlotte commented, "I'll bet this is going to cost us a fortune."

I laughed and said, "It'll be worth it." Our room was located on the front side of the hotel facing the old city of Jerusalem. The girls' room was across the hall. Charlotte and I responded to the girls' gleeful shouts early the next morning and joined them at their window, wondering what they had seen that had excited them so. The scene was breathtaking as we looked out over a panoramic view of the Israeli hillsides. A small, ancient village, perched on the side of a nearby grassy knoll, reminded me of what Bethlehem must have looked like in Jesus' day. Shepherds were tending their sheep in a valley below just as shepherds have done for thousands of years.

The girls and I couldn't wait until breakfast was over so we could visit the shepherds and take pictures. We approached an elderly Arab woman dressed in the flowing garb that shepherds have always worn. She was tending a large herd of sheep and four straggly looking children. As we walked up, she timidly shooed the sheep and children away from us. However, when I waved a dollar bill, she gave me a big, toothless smile, and they all gathered around for pictures. When we left, she and the children waved good-bye until we were out of sight.

During lunch, we were joined by Dan O'Neill, Pat Boone's son-in-law, who was there working on arrangements for the tour. When the girls happily told him about our morning's visit with the shepherds, he cautioned us to be careful where we went. Then he told us that Pat and his family had been out on that same hillside filming a Christmas television special when a sheep had gotten blown up by a land mine accidentally left from one of the wars. We decided not to go into the fields anymore, but rather, we would visit old-town Jerusalem in the afternoon.

The next day Charlotte and the girls wanted to stay around the hotel and rest up for the tour, but I was too fidgety to sit still.

I sneaked back to the hillside with my camera for more pictures. But while trying to navigate down a steep rocky slope, I slipped and went tumbling to the bottom, ending up with a badly sprained ankle. In fact, the pain was so great, I thought for a while it was broken. There was no one around to help me, so I did some serious praying. After the pain subsided a little, I exercised my faith, got up, and painfully hobbled back to the hotel. Charlotte insisted that we visit a nearby clinic, recommended by the hotel and have it x-rayed. The doctor assured me there were no broken bones, but he said that I would probably not be able to walk on it for a while.

When we got back to the hotel, I spent the rest of the day in bed with my foot packed in ice and propped on a pillow. It left me with time to reflect on my situation, "Why? Lord, why did You have to let this happen?" I complained. "You were blessing us with so much favor up until now. Why? Lord, I don't understand."

"I had to get your attention," the Lord said. "In your excitement you were running helter-skelter and not stopping to analyze why I've been giving you favor nor why I have even brought you here." I suddenly sensed that God had a serious reason for putting me on my back. I hadn't even given it a thought; our being there was Him working His will in our lives, and that was the reason we had been shown so much favor. I had just thought it was our idea of a great vacation. As I lay there continuing to meditate, I began to feel the burden of God's heart. I could sense His sorrow over the turmoil that was besieging His land, His Holy Land, and I could feel His yearning for His people— the Jews whom He had set aside from the rest of the world to be His witnesses. He'd put me on my back to get my attention, and He recruited me to be an intercessor on His behalf. A burden, His burden, was born in my heart that day, and it has never gone away.

I was up bright and early the next morning, happy to learn that my foot was much better, but I was still limping a bit as I boarded the elevator and made my way down to the hotel lobby. I was dying to meet Mr. Otis in person. As soon as the elevator doors opened, I spotted him, a small slender gentleman in his fifties with shiny white hair. He was just coming around from behind a long table that had been set up for checking in the tour members.

Mr. Otis spotted me at about the same time and came hurrying over to shake my hand as though I were a long, lost buddy. Squinting just a bit to make sure he got the name right, he said, "How are you, Captain Fish? It's so good to have you on the tour. I've been looking forward to meeting you." Then stepping back as though he had just noticed, he exclaimed, "What in the world is wrong with your foot?" A bit embarassed, I told him about my accident. After I assured him that it had been checked by a doctor, he said, "By all means, let me pray for you." Then grabbing my hands and in a loud booming voice that made me want to fall through the floor, he prayed. "Lord, heal this foot. This man has a lot of walking to do, and, Lord, we need him. May it be done in Jesus' name. Amen." When Mr. Otis said "Amen," I looked up and realized that every person in that large lobby had come to a dead standstill. It was like the "E. F. Hutton" commercial of several years ago. Then when Otis said amen, everything returned to normal as though nothing had happened. You have to realize this was an Arab-owned hotel, and the lobby was full of Arabs that I describe as sheiks dressed in flowing white robes. I had never witnessed such Christian boldness before. I decided right then that I could learn much from this man of God.

For the next six days Charlotte and I became like children ourselves, excitedly visiting all the major attractions of the Holy Land. We traveled up the Mediterranean coastline to the ancient ruins of Caesarea, where Cornelius, the first Gentile, was converted; to the modern port city of Haifa and Mount Carmel, where Elijah had his showdown with the prophets of Baal; to Megiddo, where the last great battle is to be fought; to Nazareth, where Jesus grew up; to Cana where He turned the water into wine; across the Samaria mountain range; and down to the Sea of Galilee. I'll never forget when we topped the ridge, and I caught my first glimpse of Galilee. It was more beautiful than I had imagined. However its size, seven miles wide and fourteen miles long, was much smaller than I had expected. After spending the night in a lovely hotel by the sea, we went on a boat ride across to Capernaum where Jesus performed many of His miracles. Then by bus we traveled south to where the Sea of Galilee empties into the Jordan River. There Charlotte and I, along with many others, were baptized in the Jordan.

We traveled down the Jordan Valley through Jericho, and we visited Qumran where the Dead Sea Scrolls were found. We traveled down the Dead Sea shoreline to Masada, once used by Herod for one of his magnificent palaces and a fortress. There, a group of heroic Jews committed suicide rather than fall into the hands of the Romans.

We spent our last three nights at the Diplomat Hotel and used it as a base from which to visit all the holy places around Jerusalem, Bethany, and Bethlehem. Our stay at the Diplomat was more magnificent than the first two days. This time my family was given an exclusive three-room suite adjoining one occupied by Pat Boone, his father, mother, and daughter Laura. Our daughter Lisa was so overcome by the luxurious decor of the suite that she sat down and cried. "Dad," she said, "we can't afford a place like this." We assured her that it was God's way of blessing us, and it wasn't costing us extra. In fact those first two days we were on our own hadn't cost us anything. Our rooms, our meals, our transportation, and everything had been free. Nobody would accept any money.

On the day we were to leave, we woke up to four inches of snow on the streets of Jerusalem. Traffic was at a standstill, and there were no snowplows in Jerusalem. However, we had some brave bus drivers who were willing to give it a try, and the hotel was literally kicking us all out to make room for another incoming tour. With the mass exodus of the High Adventure Tour group alone, not counting other tour groups, I knew we would fill every empty seat on every flight scheduled out of Tel Aviv. So we weren't only concerned about getting through the snow to the airport but getting a flight home once we got there. Charlotte and I both knew it would take a miracle, but we had witnessed miracles before, and we put it in God's hands.

The buses did a little slipping and sliding, but other than that, we made it to the Ben-Gurion Airport just fine. When Charlotte and the girls stepped up to the El Al check-in desk with me, the friendly agent just looked at me and smiled. "Captain Fish," she said, "With our bookings, you and your family will be lucky to get out of Israel within three days."

"But I believe in miracles," I said. "Please check our bags to New York." It took a bit of persuading to get her to do so, but she finally did agree to check all but our carry-on bags. When we got to the standby passenger lounge, we found probably close to a hundred other passengers there ahead of us who were also on standby. But somehow in spite of all the odds, I had a peace about the situation.

About ten minutes before boarding was to start, the Lord spoke to my heart. He said, "Not only will you get on this flight, but you will be seated next to Doug." Doug was an Assembly of God pastor from Oklahoma whom I had come to like. In fact, he and a Methodist pastor had baptized Charlotte and me in the Jordan River.

As I was thinking about what God had just said to me, my name was paged to come up to the standby passenger counter. There stood a smiling agent holding our five boarding passes. "It must be your lucky day, Captain Fish. I understand hundreds of passengers trying to get from Jerusalem are stranded in the snow. I'm sorry I have to split your family up, but at least you're all getting on."

First, I thanked the Lord and then said to the agent, "Thank you, and don't worry. My girls enjoy getting to know strangers. They're used to flying this way. I walked over and gave Charlotte four of the passes. At least she and Kim would be able to sit close to each other. I looked down at my seat. It was 35-D. Then I looked up and saw Doug standing on the other side of the waiting lounge. I walked over and said to him, "Doug, the Lord told me that I'll be sitting with you on the flight home."

"Oh, this sounds interesting," he said.

"What's your seat number?" I asked, and he replied, "35-E."

Then I showed him mine: 35-D. "I don't know what's happening," he said, "but this ought to be good." It was good. The miracle of our getting on a flight at all was really something, but selecting one special seat partner out of a chance of one in 430 was an even greater miracle. This made the flight time pass quickly, plus the hours and hours Doug and I spent talking about the special workings of God in our lives, our similar burden for Israel, and even discovering we had mutual friends— Tom and Lydia Crim. This was the couple who had brought the message of Pentecost to our Faith Methodist Church in Alexandria, Virginia. They had grown up in his church in Oklahoma. We landed in New York before either of us knew it.

Our Bible study group was anxiously waiting for us when we came home. Our next several Monday nights were used showing slides and reliving our tour with them. They wanted to hear every detail. Not only did we talk about the tour, we talked a lot about George Otis whom Charlotte and I had both come to love.

Sometime later, our Bible study group was again studying the Book of Revelation. In chapter 11, we were discussing our thoughts about the two witnesses mentioned in our Scripture reading. These are the two witnesses that are to appear in Jerusalem just before Christ's return. There has always been a theological debate as to who these two witnesses will be. Some say it will be Moses and Elijah. Others say it will be Enoch and Elijah. As our study group shared their own various views, the ladies asked me, "O. A., who do you think the two witnesses will be?"

Without a thought, I said, "George Otis and Pat Robertson." Everyone, including me, had a big laugh at my answer. I went on to explain that I didn't really believe they were literally the witnesses mentioned in Revelation, "But," I said, "I don't know any two men in the world today who are publicly expressing their compassion for the soul of Israel more than them." That was before there was even a hint that someday God would use them to saturate the Middle East through radio and television with the gospel of Jesus Christ.

We kept in touch with George, and I even arranged for him to speak at our local Full Gospel Businessmen's monthly dinner on March 31, 1979. On the day of George's arrival, my son-in-law, Doug Whiteside, also a pilot, flew me to the Greenville-Spartanburg Jetport where we met George's incoming commercial flight. Our flight back to the local Rutherford County Airport was smooth in the calm evening air. The sun was dipping below the horizon, causing lengthening shadows to accent our beautiful Blue Ridge Mountains. George couldn't help comparing them to the mountains of Israel. During a serene moment when we were all lost in our thoughts, I felt a tap on my shoulder. I was sitting in front with Doug, and George was in the back seat. When I turned around, he said, "O. A., you don't know it yet, but next year, you and Charlotte are going with me to the Holy Land again." Then he went on to say, "Tonight, I'm going to share something that happened this time that'll blow your socks off." When I tried to probe him for a clue, he just clammed up and smiled. He had just returned to the states from the tour. "Wait and you'll hear" is all I could get out of him.

The meeting was held in the local National Guard Armory and it was filled when we arrived. We had to hurry through the dinner because we had gotten George there a little late. Ralph shortened the preliminaries so George could have as much time as he needed to speak.

When George began speaking, his voice was strong, but after a while due to the damp, night air and sheer fatigue, he began to lose it. The acoustics in the armory were terrible; on top of that, a small infant sitting on its mother's lap up near the front began to squirm and cry, and then the cry turned into loud sobs. This made it impossible to hear George at all. When the mother made no attempt to take the baby out, George just stopped speaking and bowed his head. *What's he going to do,* I wondered. I was sitting on the platform behind him. I knew the mother, and I knew that her husband had talked her into coming with the hopes that she might come to the Lord that night. I was praying, "Lord, please don't let her have to leave."

Then George began to pray in a soft but firm voice, one that could be heard over the crying, "Lord, right now I ask that You minister peace to this mother and to this baby. Amen."

In that moment the baby looked right up into Mr. Otis' eyes and said, "Coo," then she broke into one of the most angelic smiles I've ever seen. She never let out another whimper and never took her eyes off of George for the rest of the service. It was an exciting miracle that I could hardly control my emotions.

Needless to say, it received the attention of everyone. After that, George's voice grew stronger as he got into the message he had really come to share. He said:

> This time over [to Israel], there suddenly came a call to me. The caller said that I should get a taxi and race as fast as I could to a place called **Metulla where I would meet a very important gentleman.** No Metulla is as far north as one can go and still be in Israel—right smack on the border. So I got a cab and went rocketing up there as fast as we could: I looked at my watch. Finally, we got to the place of rendezvous that was **the Arizim Hotel, a tiny hotel in Metulla with a sidewalk cafe where one** can get tea and coffee. So I got out of my taxicab and sat down there.
>
> Just about the time the caller had said it would happen, a man came up to me dressed in military garb. He had a broad face with very sad eyes. He was a man of beauty and countenance; a man I knew right away was a man to be reckoned with. I sensed the presence of God upon this military man—soft spoken, a kind of man one could look in the face and hear his words. One listens very carefully. His name was Major Saad Haddad, and he was the leader of the remaining Christians living in what he has declared to be Southern Free Lebanon. It is a narrow strip of land, barely six miles wide and seventy miles long. Pressed into the tiny strip of land are 100,000 souls—pressed up against the border of Israel. It is the determination of the Palestinian Liberation Organization and Syria, who owns and controls most of the rest of Lebanon, to destroy those Christians! So there is continual rocketing and shelling, but there is some freedom in this land tonight, and it rests on this man of God—Major Haddad.
>
> So we sat down and had coffee together, and we talked for an hour. I said, "Major, I would like to go into your sector."
>
> He said, "I can't permit you to do it, Mr. Otis, it's too dangerous."
>
> But I said, "I want to go back and be able to tell the people what I've seen, because I'm ashamed of the fact that we have all but forgotten the suffering church here. Tell me not only what your needs are, but tell me how we can pray, and what kind of report I can bring home to the Christians in America."
>
> Well, as a result of this exchange, the Major invited me to come back up in a couple of days, which I did, and that time I went into Lebanon. I met with the Christians there and testified to them, ministered to them, and heard their story.
>
> Suddenly, there came an opportunity through Major Haddad. He said, "I need a transmitter to be able to communicate with my people—the Christians who are scattered behind the PLO and Syrian lines in Beirut, Tripoli, Tyre, Sidon, and other places. If I could only communicate with

them on their little AM transistor radios, I could encourage them. We cannot communicate with any other way."

I said, "Really! Would you allow a transmitter to be put in here, right next to the Israeli border?"

He said, "I pledge to you if you get us a transmitter, we'll furnish the power, and the best security we can to see that it isn't bombed."

"Now Major," I said, "I want to really understand this. You'll give us permission to put a radio station in, and how much power can we use?"

"I don't care." he said. "I'd like a strong voice!"

Then I said to him, "Would there be anything wrong with our speaking the Word of God, playing Christian music, and giving a message now and then to the people of Syria just around the mountain, to Jordan, and to Libya across the Mediterranean? Above all, would you mind if we speak right to Israel, Jerusalem, Tel Aviv, Nazareth, Bethlehem, and Haifa?"

"Oh," he said. "That will be fine." And so we said, "In the name of Jesus we believe that within a few months you will have either a 25,000 watt or a 95,000 watt radio station setting right here on that piece of ground."

Then George directed his comments to those of us there in the armory. "I want to share with you tonight my belief. I declare to you in the name of Jesus that He will allow us within four months to key on a transmitter that will proclaim the Word of God in that troubled, peace-lacking, spiritually sterile ground that hasn't heard the voice of the Lord for much too long. To me that is the most thrilling, exciting, and moving thing I have seen in all my life!"

I rose with everyone else, applauded, and praised God with George. The thought of putting a Christian radio station in the heart of the Middle East was fantastic, but the practical side of me took over and said, *It won't work. It's too dangerous. There are too many obstacles.* I made a contribution toward the project and promised to uphold it in my prayers, but I have to admit, I had little faith that it would succeed.

The happy ending of the service should have told me that George Otis was no ordinary man, and his vision of a Christian radio station in the Middle East was no ordinary dream. Also, the miracle of the crying baby had touched its mother, and she prayed with George, asking Jesus to come into her heart.

30
Isaac's Visit

Go up to Lebanon and cry out,
let your voice be heard in Bashan,
cry out from Abarim,
for all your allies are crushed (Jer. 22:20).

The summer of '79 was a frustrating year in a lot of ways. I couldn't escape the burden of praying for the success of George Otis's impossible dream of building the radio station in Lebanon or praying for the plight of the Christians who were struggling there. But at the same time, I had a flying career to maintain and a Christian camp to operate. I kept up with the progress of the station as best I could through the High Adventure newsletters and an occasional phone call to their office in Van Nuys, California. I knew God had uniquely provided George with a radio field engineer from Toronto, Canada. His name was Paul Hunter, and he was a man of faith. I knew incredible things were happening, yet in my mind, total success for the project was too much to hope for.

Then one night while I was in a motel room during a layover, God spoke to me through a verse of scripture from Jeremiah: "Go up to Lebanon, and cry; and lift up thy voice" (KJV). The words penetrated my heart with such force that I had this word of knowledge that God's call to broadcast the Gospel from Lebanon was real. From that moment on, I knew George's commission was from God. I couldn't wait to share this verse of Scripture with him.

A few days later George called me at home. Excitedly, I told him what God had spoken to me. His response was less than I expected, "Yes, O. A., thank you for your confirmation. God has also already given me that verse, but what I really called about was to ask a favor." Then he went on to explain that he was bringing his chief Israeli tour guide, Isaac Gronberg, and his wife, Naomi, to the states for a month-long visit. He was looking for people who would host them in various parts of the country. At first I was reluctant because of our family's hectic life-style with the camp and so on, but finally I agreed we would host them for a few days.

As the day approached for the Gronbergs's arrival, Charlotte and I became a bit anxious. We'd never hosted Jewish people in our home before. We wondered if they were Orthodox Jews; if so, what would we feed them? We didn't even know where we could secure kosher food in our area. And what about the constant Christian ministry that goes on at our house? How would that affect them? With each passing day, our worry list grew longer.

When the day of their arrival came, I was out of town on a speaking engagement, so Charlotte and the girls drove to the Charlotte airport to pick them up. I couldn't wait to call Charlotte that evening to find out how it was going at home, even though I would be there early the next morning. Charlotte's giggle gave her away when she answered the phone. She was having fun. "You're going to be surprised when you meet them," she teased.

"Why's that?" I asked.

"You're going to know Isaac the minute you see him," she said.

"I am?" I quizzed. "The only tour guide I remember was on our bus, and his name was David ."

"You'll see!" was all I could get out of her.

By the time I got home the next morning, my curiosity was killing me. I went bounding up the steps of our foyer, through the kitchen, and into the den where I heard talking. And there Isaac sat, reared back in my recliner with his pretty, dark-haired wife sitting pertly on the arm. With a sweeping gesture, he yelled, "Surprise!"

Surprised, I was. Here in my home sat that big guy, the angel of mercy, who had rescued us at the Ben Gurion Airport when we had no idea where we were going to lay our heads. I couldn't believe it. We all hugged, and they talked a mile a minute, filling us in on all of the amazing coincidences they had discovered about our two families.

Charlotte said, "I recognized Isaac the moment I saw him get off the airplane in Charlotte. Then when we were getting acquainted, they mentioned that they also have three daughters, and we learned that their middle daughter, Segal, was born on the same day as our middle daughter, Lisa.

Then Isaac butted in with his somewhat broken English, "And when we was driving home, I asked Charlotte when was your anniversary?"

Charlotte jumped back in, "I said, 'February eleventh; oh, I mean July, the twenty-fifth.'"

Then it was Naomi's turn, "I said to Charlotte why did you first say February eleventh? She said, 'That's my birthday.' I squealed, 'Mine too!'"

With that discovery, they told me that the questions really began flying back and forth to learn other amazing similarities between our two families. Isaac and I had both dated our wives for three years and married within a couple months of each other. Their oldest daughter Ozly and our oldest daughter, Cheryl, had married farm boys, and they were pregnant at the same time. Our granddaughter, Jennifer, was born in September, and their grandson, Nadav, was born the following January. The similarities went on and on, so endearing us to one another that even today we regard each other as family.

We had so much fun during the days of their visit that all our worries went out the window. They even enjoyed the same food we ate.

The serious side of their visit was when I would take Isaac to speaking engagements I had lined up for him. Naomi who is a speed reader would stay home and devour the Christian testimony books in our library, just as Charlotte's dad had done when he was visiting. Listening to Isaac's stories soon led me to know that he was a man destined of God. His grandfather was a wealthy baker in Poland, but he had taken Isaac's father and his two brothers to what was then Palestine when they were young. So Isaac was born there, and he grew up helping to fight for the liberation of Israel. **He joined the Huguenots when he was** twelve; he was sixteen when the war of independence was fought over the declaration of Israel as a sovereign country in 1948. He had spent his whole life serving the Israeli army, most of it with a tank division. Therefore, he knew the sorrows of war firsthand.

I also learned of Isaac's close relationship with George Otis, and, in fact, it was he who made the necessary arrangement for George to meet Major Saad Haddad. He told me how it came about: "I was leading a tour group, and we were having lunch at a kibbutz near the Lebanon border. A friend of mine was there— he is the commanding officer of the northern Israeli troops— and he was talking to Major Haddad. I heard the major asking him: 'Can you introduce me to some Americans who might help us?' Right away I thought of George Otis, so I just went over and told my friend, 'George Otis will be here with a tour in a few weeks, he is the man for Major Haddad to meet.' I just knew it, and that's how the meeting of these two men began."

Wow, I thought as I sat spellbound listening to Isaac. No doubt, God had called him to a key role in the miracle he was performing in South Lebanon.

Another confirming sign was when Isaac said, "O. A., we just met George Otis at the airport in Tel Aviv when we were getting ready to leave for the states, and he was really excited. While coming to Israel on the plane, God had shown him a verse of scripture from Jeremiah, something about going "up to Lebanon and [crying] out" from its passages. This was the same scripture God had given me in the motel to confirm in my own spirit that the call to Lebanon was truly from Him. Then Isaac said something else that showed me the timing was right for bringing the gospel broadcast into Israel: "Israel is in a state of national repentance. She now has begun to realize that all her problems throughout her tumultuous history have occurred because of turning her back on God."

Repentance! I thought, *that's the key to her awakening.* After all, wasn't that the message of John the Baptist, forerunner of Jesus' ministry on earth?

God truly used Isaac and Naomi's visit to enlighten me more as to the workings of His sovereign grace. We were sad when we had to say good-bye to them at the airport.

"Next year, Jerusalem!" we shouted as we waved.

31

Tribute to Charbel Younes

In a very short time, will not Lebanon
be turned into a fertile field
and the fertile field seem like a forest?
In that day the deaf will hear the
words of the scroll,
and out of gloom and darkness
the eyes of the blind will see.
Once more the humble will rejoice in the Lord;
the needy will rejoice in the Holy One of Israel (Isa. 29:17-19).

After Isaac's visit, our summer went so fast I couldn't keep up with all that was happening with the "Voice of Hope" project. I knew that in mid-August Paul Hunter, the field engineer, and a crew of technicians had arrived in Lebanon along with the equipment to begin work. I had also heard how they were being hampered by bombings from the PLO's Beaufort Castle stronghold. I guess I had figured it would take months to complete the project. So, somehow I missed it when every major news network in the world made the announcement that the Voice of Hope was signing on the air September 9, 1979.

My exposure to the news came as a complete surprise one evening when I turned on the TV to watch ABC's "20/20" report. Just as I turned the set on, Geraldo Rivera was reporting, "The Nation of Lebanon is not merely divided; it is completely shattered—torn to pieces by fighting."

I became totally fixed to the television set. I plopped down on the floor to watch and listen as Geraldo went on reporting about

the different factions and hot spots of Lebanon, and then he ze-
roed in on Southern Free Lebanon. He showed pictures of Beaufort Castle, the old crusader-built edifice, that had been turned
into a stronghold by the PLO. He told how they used it to bring
devastation with their machine guns, cannons, and rockets on
Major Haddad's enclave and northern Israel. Then he interviewed Major Haddad. It was the first time I had seen the Major.
His blazing black eyes and tightly set jaw gave him an appearance of toughness. But when he began to speak in a soft low
voice, his whole countenance changed. He spoke as a man pos-
sessed with compassion for his suffering people. Geraldo then
moved on to say, "Well, in one of the most unusual twists in the
fortunes of war, this frequent battleground is now the headquar-
ters of a most unusual radio station."

The ABC cameras then focused on the old, shell-pocked
French customs building that had been converted into a studio.
The twin, 250-foot broadcast towers were situated just north of
the studio. I almost stopped breathing when Geraldo began to
interview George Otis who was sitting behind a WORD microphone. "Why did you locate your station here in such a hot
spot?" Geraldo asked.

"Well," said George, "we believe where maximum trouble
and maximum abandonment by the rest of the Christian world
existed was a place where we needed to come, so we set up a
25,000-watt AM gospel station to pour out the word of God and
bring encouragement."

"Do you think the Christians here have been abandoned by
the outside Christian world?" Geraldo asked.

"I know they have!" said George. "And I felt so ashamed
when I found out there had been nearly a genocide of the Christian population in free Lebanon, and they had really been saved
by the Jewish People."

As Geraldo continued his report I was almost raptured with
joy at the faithfulness of our God. As soon as "20/20" was
over, I reached George by phone at his home in Van Nuys, California, to tell him how much the story had meant to me.

From that day on, I knew beyond any doubt that the destiny of
south Lebanon was firmly in the hands of God, and I became

gripped by a spirit of intercession for Major Haddad, the station, the Lebanese Christians, and for the spiritual awakening of Israel. But I not only prayed, I lent myself to the work as best I could by giving and publicizing it through every medium that opened to me—talking to individuals and groups on radio and television and writing to newspapers, politicians, and government agencies. Our Monday night Bible study also began praying and supporting the High Adventure ministry. Sue Hardin, Carolyn Curtis, and Juanita Randal—ladies from our study group—joined my family and several others from our county on a tour of Israel plus a visit into south Lebanon to see the station the following February in 1980.

On that visit, I met Paul Hunter's Lebanese counterpart: Charbel Younes, a self-taught radio engineer, and Major Saad Haddad. On subsequent visits when Charlotte and I would travel there to minister and offer our encouragement to the Voice of Hope staff, we developed a deep love for Charbel, a little man in stature but a giant man in God's kingdom. I had such a desire to share the story of Charbel with the rest of the world I wrote an article about him that was published in *Power for Living* (July 7, 1985, Scripture Press Publications, Inc. Used by permission).

"Praise de Lord!"
A Voice of Hope for Lebanon

Lebanon, once the "garden spot of the Middle East," is today known as a land of black-robed widows and wailing orphans. The little country has been savagely torn by warring factions. Yet amid the cruel fighting, a sound of hope is being heard. It is a powerful gospel radio station called the Voice of Hope, and it is bringing the Good News of Jesus Christ to a dim corner of the earth.

The spark of Hope was struck in the heart of a young Lebanese Christian named Charbel Younes. A radio-television repairman before the war, Charbel lives with his wife Maureena and their four children in Merj 'Uyun, a village, in south Lebanon. Only 5'2" tall, but built like a football player, Charbel has a quick smile; his green eyes are gentle, yet piercing behind black-rimmed glasses. His favorite broken-English expression: "Praise de Lord!"

Charbel remembers the dark days of 1978, when continual attacks by the Palestine Liberation Organization (PLO) against his Christian enclave had broken the spirit of his people. For the enclave—several villages with a combined population of about 35,000—the situation seemed hopeless. The people were afraid to assemble for fear of terrorists; their telephone and mail systems had been destroyed, cutting them off from the outside world; and sniper fire kept them from working their fields, so that crops were failing, and many had to go to bed hungry.

The enclave's only earthly hope seemed to rest on the shoulders of a military man, Major Saad Haddad. But his poorly equipped 2,000-man militia was heavily outnumbered by PLO forces that had cut him off from the rest of Lebanon.

It was then that Charbel began to construct a homemade transmitter out of used radio and television parts. When it was finished, it had a broadcast range of only one mile. But Charbel used it to play happy music, and Major Haddad would speak encouragement over the airwaves to the few people able to tune in.

Major Haddad was grateful for Charbel's efforts. But he would longingly say, "Charbel, we must have a stronger voice! Without a voice we will perish!"

God had given Charbel talent, but what he needed now was parts. He prayed that God would supply him with a modulator tube, which could increase his transmitter's range by several miles.

In February 1979 came a glimmer of hope. A Christian from California who was leading a tour of Israel wanted to meet with the major. Would he be able to provide Charbel with his needed tube? The man was evangelist George Otis, a former executive with the Lear Corporation who harbored a burning desire to reach the Middle East for Christ.

Otis was moved by the Lebanese men's humble request for a modulator tube. So moved, in fact, that his reply was a shout: "A small transmitter? Why not build a powerful gospel radio station that can reach the entire Middle East?"

Taken back by the American's boldness, Major Haddad stammered, "Well, ah, that would be fine—but, remember, we are situated in a hot battle area." He didn't know how seriously to take the small, white-haired evangelist who sat before him.

Otis countered as though he hadn't heard the major's last remark. "Then we will build it!" he declared. "We will build it in the name of the Living God!"

News of that meeting spread throughout the area. But few, if any, believed a radio station could be built—and survive—in such a hostile area. Even Charbel doubted.

A few weeks later, however, Otis was back with Paul Hunter, a radio field engineer from Canada. A field survey was completed, and the picturesque Valley of the Springs was selected as an ideal broadcast site—

just a couple of miles from Metula, Israel's most northern outpost village.

Soon thousands of Christians in the United States and Canada were contributing money to build the station. By mid-August, construction began.

But the sounds of hammers and saws were not the only ones in the valley. Barrages of rocket and canon fire from the PLO's Beaufort Castle stronghold were coming in on the workers. The old castle, perched on a high bluff, gave a bird's-eye view of the construction site only seven miles away.

Yet in spite of the shelling, the hot summer sun, and primitive working conditions, the men kept on with the task. Charbel became a sort of shadow to Paul Hunter, and his faith and courage gave strength to the workers who labored from dawn to dark. Then, on the fifth day of work, God granted an answer to prayer as a mysterious explosion blew the top floor off Beaufort Castle and sent it toppling into the river below. Shelling ceased until the project was completed. Within just four weeks, the dedicated crew of workers had the Voice of Hope signing on the air. Twin 200-foot antennas had been erected; hundreds of miles of copper wire, radiating from the bases of the towers, had been buried; two diesel-powered AM transmitters were installed in a deserted, concrete pump house; and a bomb-scarred, old French customs house had been reno-vated into a modern broadcast studio.

On September 9, 1979, the station's first message was hurled into the heavens; "Jesus Christ is Lord! Jesus is Lord, and He is coming back soon. You are listening to WORD, the Voice of Hope radio station, lo-cated in the Valley of the Springs, south Lebanon." Charbel became resi-dent engineer for the station.

In time WORD's daily 18-hour format came to include gospel and country music, hourly newscasts, locally generated programs, children's Bible stories, biblical teachings, and 60-second Bible readings every 15 minutes. The *Jerusalem Post* dubbed the latter "commercials from God."

A mix of languages was chosen in an effort to serve the station's varied listeners. Bible readings and most news went out in English, directed mainly toward Israel; Arabic and French programs were beamed for the Lebanese; even some Russian programming was added, along with a shortwave transmitter called the "King of Hope," KING, which blankets Europe, Asia, the Soviet Union, and some of Africa. Later an FM trans-mitter was added, and then a VHF color television station. Later George Otis, president of High Adventure Ministries of Van Nuys, California, listened to the Lord's directing, and gave the television station he had birthed to the Christian Broadcasting Network of Virginia Beach, Virgin-ia, that is headed by Pat Robertson.

The Voice of Hope began to bring exactly that to the Lebanese people. Even the weather changed; rain began falling after years of drought, which residents took as a sign from God. They were no longer afraid to work in their fields, and in spite of continued terrorist activities, began making repairs to their shell-pocked buildings.

Charbel tells visitors how God has protected the station. He tells of carrying off live shells in wire baskets; the shells landed close but never exploded. He also says local people gather at the station when the shellings start—knowing they will be safe there.

Considering that the nearest Radio Shack store is thousands of miles away, it's been quite a feat for the Lord and Charbel to have kept the station operating with mostly make-to-do parts. At this writing, the Voice of Hope hasn't missed a day of broadcasting. The staff lavishes Charbel with compliments, but he just shrugs and says, "Praise de Lord!"

Sometimes the Lord uses unexpected sources to provide Charbel with spare parts. Consider this story told by Chuck Pollack, the station manager: "When Israel moved into south Lebanon to force the PLO out, fighting was fierce, and we were broadcasting around the clock. Charbel became in need of a special electronic shielded connector, and we searched all over Israel without finding one.

"Meanwhile, an Israeli fighter plane shot down a Russian-built Syrian MIG, and its tail section fell nearby. Harold Cox, one of our staff, dragged the tail to the studio, and Charbel began stripping out its electronic components. We all went running outside when we heard him shouting, "Praise de Lord! . . . Praise de Lord!" We discovered that there in the MIG's tail section, he had found the very electronic connector he needed!"

Thus Charbel Younes and his colleagues trust the Lord to hold the station together. Recently Charbel turned down a high-salaried teaching job offered by his government. He chose instead to continue his mission with the Voice of Hope for much less money—and to bring the glory of God to the troubled Middle East.

I sent copies of the *Power for Living* article to Charbel in hopes of encouraging him, but I didn't hear from him. Then recently Brother Otis flew Charbel to the states, his first time out of the Middle East, and I met him in California. Charbel recognized me right away and threw his arms around me. "Charbel," I asked, "Did you get the article I sent you?"

"Yes," he said with a wide grin, "I made copies and passed it out all over south Lebanon, and I say to the people, 'See, there are Christians who know about us, and they care.' " That grin made all the effort I had put into the article worthwhile.

As was mentioned in the Charbel article, the television station pioneered by George Otis High Adventure was turned over to Pat Robertson of the Christian Broadcasting Network. Even though George knew in his heart it was the thing to do, he said that giving the TV station away was like giving up a child he had birthed.

George didn't quite understand it at the time, but now sees his ministry is to reach the world with shortwave. Added to the Middle East stations is KVOH, Voice of Hope for the Americas based in Van Nuys. It is beamed across South America and reaches over 70 countries. Added to the Middle East stations is another shortwave transmitter beamed at Africa, and soon another station will go on the air in Guam with a strong signal beamed at China. With the stations linked together, every short wave receiver in the world will be able to tune in a Voice of Hope broadcast.

Pat Robertson has done wonders with what is now the Middle East broadcasting television network, broadcasting gospel television to a large segment of the Middle East.

Recently, I was speaking to the New Life Assembly Church in Conover, North Carolina, and I was talking about the Voice of Hope station in Lebanon. There was a Jewish couple in the congregation. They were bright eyed as I spoke, so I couldn't wait to talk with them after the service. They had just moved to the United States from Tel Aviv. When I asked them if they had listened to the Voice of Hope station, they replied "No, we didn't know about it until tonight, but we both accepted the Lord after watching the "700 Club" on the Middle East Television Network." They had started watching the program, thinking at first it was another soap opera, and then they said, "We found it was for real." They also said, "All of our friends in Tel Aviv are hooked on it." Truly, the words of the Book are coming out of Lebanon, and the eyes of the blind are being opened.

Once when I was visiting in the home of Isaac and Naomi just outside of Tel Aviv, they tuned in the Voice of Hope shortwave signal so I could hear the excellent quality of its signal. Just as

the station came in on the dial, Alexander Scorby was reading
Isaiah 55:10-11:

> "As the rain cometh down, and the snow from heaven, and returneth
> not thither, but watereth the earth, and maketh it bring forth and bud,
>   . . . So shall my word be that goeth forth out of my mouth: it shall not
> return unto me void, but it shall accomplish that which I please, and it
> shall prosper in the thing whereto I sent it." (KJV)

I looked over at Naomi and noticed tears trickling off her
cheeks. The Spirit spoke to my heart and said, "This type of
thing is happening all over the Middle East." It humbles me to
think that God has privileged me to have a tiny part in planting
the seed that is bringing forth this fruit.

32

In Loving Memory of Major Saad Haddad

All these people were still living by faith when they died. They did not receive the things promised; they only saw them and welcomed them from a distance. And they admitted that they were aliens and strangers on earth. People who say such things show that they are looking for a country of their own. If they had been thinking of the country they had left, they would have had opportunity to return. Instead, they were longing for a better country—a heavenly one. Therefore God is not ashamed to be called their God, for he has prepared a city for them (Heb. 11:13-16).

These Scriptures, of course, refer to the promise of hope to the list of Old Testament heroes named in Hebrews 11. I'm sure God's list of heroes is still expanding, and on that list you will surely find Major Saad Haddad.

On Saturday, January 14, 1984, Major Saad Haddad, the Lebanese Christian military leader allied with Israel, died of cancer at his home in Mar Jayoun, south Lebanon. He was forty-eight and a bone-weary soldier who, even during his illness, gave the last drop of his energies to help relieve the sufferings of his people. Besides being a servant and soldier, perhaps his greatest contribution to all Christians was in providing the opportunity for Christian radio and television to come to the Middle East.

On the day of my last visit with Major Haddad in 1982, Chuck Pollak, station manager of the Voice of Hope radio station, picked me up in Metulla to drive me to the Major's home. We crossed the border at the "Good Fence" checkpoint situated at the outskirts of Metulla and proceeded along the ridgetop of a small mountain range on which Mar Jayoun is situated—five miles north of the Israeli border. Along the narrow, blacktopped road filled with potholes caused by war, millions of wild flowers thrived amidst war-strewn debris where houses once stood. It was a clear, crisp spring day, and our eyes feasted on an aerial view of the lush fertile Valley of the Springs on our right. The valley was named for its many springs which are fed by the melting snow of Mount Hermon that rises majestically into the eastern sky. Right in the middle of the valley, we could see the renovated old Customs building housing the Voice of Hope studio. The studio gave one a comforting feeling in knowing that this building, finely structured to house the French customs during their period of occupation in the early forties and deserted to become a stable for sheep and goats, had finally been reclaimed as the birthplace for a gospel broadcast station. From that spot the "tidings of great joy, which shall be to all people" (Luke 2:10, KJV) was being broadcast day and night. The whole valley seemed vibrant and alive, beautifully attesting to the fingerprints of God.

However on the left, the scene was totally different. The difference was like day and night, like life and death. Rough, barren terrain dropped sharply down into the Litani River gorge and then rose from the other side of the river in steep-browing cliffs. Perched on the highest peak of these cliffs, like a giant wart, loomed the hulking ruins of Beaufort Castle—the fortress God had silenced so His servants could complete work on the station. The PLO terrorists had converted the old Crusader-built castle into an almost impenetrable fortress. Its fifteen-foot-thick rock walls which had withstood centuries of time had mockingly repelled the cannon fire of Major Haddad's World War II tanks. Beaufort's threat had struck terror in the hearts of Christians and Israelis alike who unfortunately lived within the 20-mile range of their Russian-built cannons and rockets. Its evil appearance merely caused me to shudder.

We passed through Kleah, another small, war-scarred Christian village and soon reached Mar Jayoun. After maneuvering through several rutted, narrow, winding streets and alleys, Chuck pulled over and stopped. "This is it," he stated, nodding to a small house across the street. But my attention was so fixed on an army vehicle, parked nose to nose with us, that I hardly heard him. The newly painted, metallic-gray war machine was a refurbished World War II-tracked personnel carrier with a 50-caliber machine gun mounted on top. Painted on the left-front armored hull was a "Star of David," signifying that it had been supplied by Israel, but the decals juxtaposed on the front loading hatch that riveted my attention.

Below a picture of the Major was a life-size picture of the face of Jesus and another picture of Mary and the Christ child—the symbol of God's love mounted on a war machine. The thought left me nauseated. Perhaps most American Christians who take their religious freedom for granted would have felt the same way. As I sat there pondering the paradoxical scene before me, goose bumps suddenly ran up and down my arms, and they weren't caused by the chilly March air but from Jesus' words which were flooding into my mind, "Do not suppose that I have come to bring peace to the earth. . . . but a sword" (Matt. 10:34). Then I remembered words that I had heard Major Haddad speak, "You may think that Christians shouldn't fight, and I agree, they shouldn't fight. However, there comes a time when we must fight! We must fight to protect the lives of our families and our property, and most of all we must fight to protect our religious freedom." Then he would say, "We are not just fighting the PLO and Syrians, but we are fighting the devil, himself!"

Then more words of Jesus came to my mind, "Upon this rock I will build my church; and the gates of hell shall not prevail against it" (Matt. 16:18, KJV). It then dawned on me that we were at that moment just a few miles from the slopes of Mount Hermon where Jesus had uttered that declaration, and at the same time we were just a few miles from the ancient city of Tyre—the city that the prophets compared with evil. In fact, Ezekiel alludes to Satan being the king of Tyre (28:11-19). *Surely,* I thought, *if there is such a place on earth, this must be the gates of hell.* The realization struck me that these Christians of Lebanon represent the only sizable surviving Christian population in the Middle East: The place where Christianity began. "Can the Christian population survive this hostile place?" I mused to myself. My head told me there was no way, but my heart told me they must. If Jesus' words are to ring true, they must!

We sat there in Chuck's car for several minutes without either
of us saying a word. It was like he understood the wrenching that
was tearing my soul. I continued to reflect on the tumultuous
history of the Lebanese Christians. Because of my keen burden
for the area, I had studied it well. For centuries, the Christians
here had survived mass onslaughts of Islamic terror. Time and
time again, the rest of the world had come to their rescue. That's
why the French had been there, to fill the role as protectorate
until Lebanon became a sovereign democratic state in 1948.
The Christians' existence in Lebanon is a source of grievous em-
barrassment to their Muslim neighbors, and along with the
flames of fervent Islamic revival stirring, many of the fanatical
Muslim groups are vowing that this situation will change.

Chuck finally interrupted, "O. A.," he said, "I hate to disturb
your thoughts, but we must not keep the Major waiting." The
Major's home was a flat roofed, stuccoed, single-family dwelling
that was common in the area. As we strolled across the street, I
was struck by the lack of security, because I knew the Major has
many enemies. A personnel carrier was parked out front, and
two militia sentries were in an empty storefront. Spanning the
width of the house were wooden ammunition crates that had
been filled with sand and stacked to the ceiling.

Standing in the doorway to greet us was the Major. He looked
even shorter than the 5'6" height he was reported to be, and I
judged him to weigh about 150 pounds. He nervously rubbed
his hand over his balding forehead and gave us a tight-lipped
smile as he graciously welcomed us into his home.

The living room we entered was very chilly, adding to the seriousness that was so prevalent. A dingy bulb hanging from the
ceiling provided the only light. The single, drapeless, front window had been covered by the ammunition crates. The modest
rectangular room was painted pastel gray. A rust-colored tweed
carpet that smelled of mildew covered the floor, and the other
skimpy furnishings consisted of two upholstered sofas: One
placed against the front wall, where Chuck and I were invited to
sit, and the other against the back wall. A walnut-stained coffee
table sat bare in the middle of the floor, and a decorative two-
tiered end table, that seemed out of place, sat in the left corner

of the room, adorned with a fancy lace doily and a beautiful Oriental vase. The Major's makeshift office was crowded in the front-left corner of the room. It consisted of a small square table that was draped with a chocolate brown-and-white-floral table cloth and a straight-back chair. The table was cluttered with several two-way radios, a military field telephone, and the picture of a much-younger Haddad, proudly dressed in a neatly starched khaki uniform. Other army paraphernalia was scattered about, and several clear plastic bags served as file cabinets.

The Major, who sat in his straight-back chair across from us, was dressed in clean but faded army fatigues with yellowish maple leaves stenciled onto the epaulets. A thin, blond mustache accented his round, bronze-tanned face. He spoke softly in broken English, and I had to lean forward and listen carefully to understand what he was saying. He had learned English while attending military training stateside at Fort Benning, Georgia.

Major Haddad was among a small band of Lebanese soldiers who were forced to flee to Beirut when his native Mar Jayoun was overrun by the PLO in March of '76. The PLO commandeered the area in south Lebanon after fleeing from Jordan and the wrath of King Hussein's fierce, fighting Bedouin soldiers. However, Major Haddad had come back to his native area, and with the help of Israel in 1978, he pushed the PLO out of the five- to ten-mile strip of land that bordered Israel. This caused Selim al-Hoss, Lebanon's Muslim prime minister at the time, to brand him as a traitor. Selim had accused Haddad of deserting the Lebanese regular army. Even the American press had largely agreed. This was one question I had been yearning to ask the Major: "Is there any substance to these accusations?" When I did, he squinted his eyes and tightened his jaws; it was apparent this was a sore subject for him.

"No-o-o," he drawled. "You must realize our country was being torn apart by civil wars. Our army began to disintegrate—the Muslims divided against the Christians. Two officers, who were brothers, were in charge of this area, but they were afraid for their lives and refused to stay because of the Syrian backed PLO.

My government asked for volunteers, so I accepted the assignment. Victor Hung, the Lebanese chief of staff, gave me my orders which had come from President Suleiman Franjeh. Already a relationship had begun with Israel, so for my safety—because the territory between Beirut and here was controlled by the PLO and Syrians—they had to send me by boat to Haifa, Israel, and from there the Israelis took me safely back to Mar Jayoun."

"Major Haddad," I then said, "tell me in your own words what the living conditions were like for the Christians here when you returned."

A pained expression came over him, he took a deep breath and slowly blew it out. "What I found was very bad," he began. "Some of the people had no bread to eat. Many went to bed hungry. People couldn't work in their fields. We are farmers, you know. Nothing! All they cared to do was protect their lives. It's very hard. I don't like to remember."

Then after a long pause to gain his composure, the Major continued, "I had to do something, so I turned to Israel and asked them for help. At first they gave us food and medical help; our doctors had all been killed or run off. The area was disorganized, and the Christians had no defense. They could be attacked very easily. So I formed a militia, and later Israel began to help us militarily. At first, they only supplied us with small arms and ammunition."

There was more and more hesitation in the Major's voice as he continued to talk. He seemed to be searching the motive of his own soul. He said, "I don't know if I've done right. I don't know. Only God can tell."

This so-called holy war was not only a paradox for me, but for the Major as well. He wore the uniform of a soldier, but his heart ached for peace. He talked of his yearning for Lebanon once again to be united and free from aggression and free to worship God according to the dictates of their own hearts. The determination I saw in the Major's firm, square jaw told me that he could settle for nothing less.

The aroma of fresh-baked bread drifted in from the kitchen where Theresa, his wife, was preparing the evening meal. From the basement—the safest place in the house—came muffled sounds of children chattering in Arabic. The Major had five daughters and one on the way. It made me sad to realize there was no sound of laughter. It was a time of seriousness, a time of war.

Suddenly, I felt an urgent desire to cheer the Major up, so I changed the subject. "Major," I said, "Christians everywhere owe you a debt of gratitude for bringing Christian broadcasting to this dark part of the world."

His eyes became shiny, and the first hint of a smile crossed his face as he became talkative again. "Yes, this is the first time the Christian voice is being heard in Lebanon, and I am proud of it. Even if I disappeared, I feel I have achieved something. At least, I let the voice of Christianity be heard in the Middle East which is empty of Christians. It is really something unbelievable. I was praying about a radio station, and we have a man who has some knowledge: Charbel Younes. He managed to fabricate one that would broadcast one kilometer." The Major laughed. "What a joke! We prayed for Charbel a big tube, but we didn't find one. After I met George Otis at the Arizim hotel, we were talking about the situation. He asked me, and I told him we needed to get our voice out. He came up with the idea. I didn't believe really that he would do it, because before him many persons gave promises that they didn't keep. But I found him to be serious, and the miracle came true. I tell you—George Otis—you can call him the "miracle man."

Some of the news media in the states were referring to the Voice of Hope as a "rebel radio station" and a "platform of propaganda for Major Haddad." I was curious to get his reaction to such reports. I told him what the press had reported and asked, "How do you feel about this?"

Again there was a pained expression; but before he could answer, Chuck Pollak, who had remained quiet up to this point chimed in. "Only on rare occasions," exclaimed Chuck, "has the Major ever used the station to address political matters, but there have been a number of times that he has used it as a pulpit—once last spring after a two-month drought had hit the land, and the farmers were in bad shape. That's when the Major showed up at the Voice of Hope and requested to go on the air.

Holding the mike, he said, 'Our God is a God of miracles. He cares about our needs,' and then he began to pray: 'God, we ask in the name of Jesus that You have mercy on us. Many, many times You have answered our prayers. Today, we must have rain for our sorely needed crops to grow, and so, we pray that You will give us this rain. Amen!' "

As Chuck told the story, I was moved to tears. I remembered how at the Arizim, a number of locals had told me about the startling results of that particular broadcast. "Within hours after the Major had prayed," they said, "it had been clear; then, suddenly, out of nowhere clouds rolled in and brought a downpour, and it hasn't been dry since."

As my visit with Major Haddad came to a close, I realized more than ever the heavy responsibility and burden that rested on his shoulders, his deep hurt because he cared so much, and the dependence he placed on God as he confessed his own inadequacy. I recalled the Old Testament Book of Judges in which time after time the children of Israel found themselves oppressed by their enemies, and they cried out to God. The Scripture says, "The Lord raised them up a deliverer" (3:15, KJV). Major Haddad was without a doubt God's modern-day answer to the cries of South Lebanese Christians.

The next time I saw Major Haddad was on the national news. The Israeli forces had moved into Lebanon, pushed the PLO out of the south, and captured Beaufort Castle. They made a formal presentation of the castle to Major Haddad. I wept as the television cameras whirred, recording the Major and his men happily hoisting the Lebanese flag above Beaufort's ruins. It had to have been one of the Major's finest hours.

The last great honor bestowed on him just before his death was when Lebanon's President Amin Gemayel reinstated him and his militia into the regular Lebanese army.

In tribute to my good friend, the Major, I say, "Farewell, Christian soldier, you fought a good fight, and now the battle is ours. May God take our loss and make it heaven's gain."

33
Challenger's Fate Impacts My Life

They that wait upon the Lord shall renew their strength; they shall mount up with wings as eagles (Isa. 40:31, KJV).

The biggest struggle of my Christian walk was always trying to discipline myself to wait upon the Lord. Yet, I knew when I took the time to invoke God's blessings and wait for His answers, those were always the times I profited most from life. Throughout my airline career, I'd tried to remember to pray before the start of each flight and to ask God for His divine protection. But there came a period when I wasn't faithful in doing that. Perhaps, God was looking after me so well that I began to take His blessings for granted. But whatever the cause, it didn't take long for Him to shake some sense back in me.

It was a snowy winter evening in Boston. We were making our approach into the Boston Logan International Airport, and Barney Ross, my copilot, and I were flying a Boeing 757, the most technically advanced airliner in the world at that time. As we descended below eight thousand feet, we hit some rough turbulence. I looked at Barney who was doing the flying and said, "Boy, I'm sure glad we're leading the pack tonight." It was the typical evening rush hour for flights getting into Boston, and we were number one of about twenty flights working the Boston Approach Control.

We were still bouncing along at four thousand feet while being vectored over the airport for a landing on Runway 22 Left. Just as we were crossing over the airport, there was a sudden wind change, and our approach was switched to land on Runway

31. The approach controller vectored us in tight for our new runway in order to cut down the delay for the flights behind us. Even though Barney and I were experienced on the B-757, we didn't have time to make the necessary changes to the computers and radios that we needed to in order to make a safe approach. So, reluctantly, I informed the controller that we needed to be vectored for a new approach. This meant going to the back of the pack and twenty more minutes of bouncing around. But, eventually, we were once again on final approach. This time everything was looking good until we came down to about three hundred feet, and I noticed a dark shadow on the takeoff end of the runway. I couldn't be sure what it was. I strained my eyes to see past the brightly lit approach lights and blowing snow. Barney was looking at the instruments, as he should, when suddenly I yelled, "Go around! There's another plane on the runway!"

At the same moment, the tower realized what had happened. The visibility was so bad that they hadn't noticed the other plane still on the runway. "Cleared for immediate takeoff!" the tower operator shouted to him while in the same breath instructing us to go around. There were a few more tense moments before we were sure we were clear of the departing aircraft and another twenty minutes before we could get vectored back into position for a final safe landing.

So by the time we got to the hotel that night, I was totally exhausted. I fell across the bed, but it was some time before I could unwind and go to sleep. "Why did You permit this to happen, Lord?" I asked. "For so long now, You've blessed my flights and allowed things to go smoothly."

Then came that still small voice, "You didn't ask me for a smooth flight." Guilt pierced me as I realized that I had let my fellowshiping with God wax cold. Indeed, I had not prayed about that flight. In fact, I had gradually taken on the attitude toward God of "watch me," instead of "help me."

I asked God to forgive me and help me to remember to wait upon Him. Then I made an unusual request of God. I prayed, "Lord, tomorrow, I want You to use my life to somehow be a witness to thousands—I don't know how—but that's the desire of my heart." Then I fell into a restful sleep.

The next morning, I awoke with the sun glistening on new-fallen snow. It was a bright sunny morning in Boston, January 28, 1986—a day that will long be remembered. Soon I was back at the airport preparing for the next leg of my flight sequence—a nonstop flight from Boston to Miami. I had forgotten about the scheduled space shuttle flight of Challenger, until I picked up my dispatch release and saw that my routing to Miami had been changed.

The following story of what happened next was published in *Guideposts* magazine, September 1986, and later in *Reader's Digest:*

"39,000 Feet Over Florida"

Normally, on the Eastern Airlines Boston-Miami flight that I captain we follow the East Coast to Wilmington, North Carolina, then go down Atlantic Route 1, a shortcut to Miami over water. But on the morning of January 28, that route would have taken us 60 miles east of Cape Canaveral and into the flight pattern of the space shuttle, Challenger. So, when I took my place at the controls of our Boeing 757, I was not surprised that we had been rerouted to stay over land and fly down the coastline airway.

We had 135 passengers on board and were ready to go, but the delay in launching the Challenger was delaying us too. From time to time on the intercom I tried to keep the passengers informed as to the reasons for the holdup. I expected some to grumble, irritated at the time loss; however, for once everyone seemed to understand. They were interested in this particular launching, especially because it was to carry the first civilian into space, school teacher Christa McAuliffe.

At last we received permission to take off, and for a while the flight went according to plan. Just south of Wilmington, however, there was a change. Air Traffic Control had just turned us off course on a radar vector saying it was for "spacing" when I heard one of the other pilots on the frequency ask, "Did the spacecraft take off yet?"

There was a pause. Then came the controller's answer. "Yes . . . but . . it blew up one minute into flight."

Stunned silence on the frequency.

Then someone broke in, "Did you just say what I thought you said?"

"Yes, I'm afraid so."

My copilot, Barney Ross, and I sat there staring into the open space ahead of us, not speaking at first. Then the words began to stumble out. "No!"

"It can't be . . . not all those people . . ."

"I don't believe it!"

Halting, inadequate expressions of disbelief and denial. Then slowly we each drifted back into our own private silence.

My thoughts turned to our passengers. How would the news affect them? Then I remembered how Boston was a regional airport for the Northeast. There might be friends or relatives of Christa McAuliffe on the plane. I couldn't make an announcement like that cold over the PA system. It wasn't like a weather report or a landmark below.

But what was I supposed to do? I had a small community of people back there who deserved to know. Yet how could I know what kind of effect it would have on them? If I had been back home, I would have known what to do. I would have prayed with my friends and members from my church. But that was different. There in my own community close to the people I knew, we could have reached out to God for comfort and assurance. But this was a Boeing 757 filled with people I'd never seen before.

Should I tell them or wait until we landed? Barney and Mary Pipe, the senior flight attendant, thought I should wait. While I was still trying to decide, a note was handed to me from a passenger, a medical doctor from South America. He was complimenting our entire crew on the flight. He said we had done a superb job and that he particularly liked the way I had kept them informed about what was going on with the space shuttle and the reasons for the delay.

Barney tapped me on the shoulder. I looked up from the note, my eyes following his gaze out the cockpit window. There was a large cloud, a white vapor giant standing starkly against the naked blue Florida sky. It was different from normal clouds. I knew it was the one formed by the spacecraft explosion. In the past I had asked God to help me minister to people during times of need on my flights, and this was one of those times. I'd have to trust Him to help me.

Suddenly, I realized I had a doctor on board. Did I also have a minister? I turned and ask Mary to check. She was back moments later. Yes, **the Reverend J. D. Gauthier, a Jesuit priest, was seated near the rear.**

"Go back and call him and the doctor aside," I told her. "Tell them the news and ask if they would be willing to assist should we need them."

Mary came back soon and said that both men were deeply moved and would help. They agreed that I should make the announcement. "And," she said, "Reverend Gauthier has offered to say a prayer afterwards, if you wish?"

I glanced once more out the window as the ominous cloud drew nearer, then turned back to Mary, "Thanks," I said. "He is the answer to my prayer. We'll do it."

I picked up the microphone and switched it on. "Ladies and gentlemen, I have some very distressing news," I began. "I'm sorry to have to tell you . . . but the spacecraft Challenger . . . has been destroyed . . ." I struggled to force the words out. "It exploded just after takeoff."

We were over Daytona Beach, and as I banked the plane, the huge cloud floated up into the passenger's view. I switched off my mike as Father Gauthier began reading the twenty-third Psalm over the flight attendant's PA system.

"The Lord is my Shepherd; there is nothing I shall want. Fresh and green are the pastures where He gives me repose," he read, "Near restful waters He leads me . . ." By now we were passing over Cape Canaveral, and we could see a long dark snakelike stain stretching out over the ocean, probably the residue of the fuel that wasn't burned.

"[The reading continued:] ". . . to revive my dropping spirit. He guides me along the right paths; He is true to His name. If I should walk in the valley of darkness . . ." The shadow of the huge cloud had fallen across the plane by now, blocking the sun.

" . . . no evil would I fear. You are there with Your crook and Your staff; with these You give me comfort. You have prepared a banquet for me in the sight of my foes. My head You have anointed with oil; my cup is overflowing . . ." As the cloud passed from sight, sunlight once again streamed through the windows. "Surely goodness and kindness shall follow me all the days of my life. In the Lord's house shall I dwell for ever and ever."

Father Gauthier prayed for the astronauts, for their families. Even though I couldn't see them from the cockpit, I knew that every head on our plane was bowed and every heart touched.

After we'd landed in Miami, I left the cockpit as soon as possible to meet the man whose prayer had helped us all. As I looked at Father Gauthier standing beside me, I thought how different he was from my small-town Assembly of God preacher at home—and yet how alike in his concern for others.

Together we watched the passengers disembark. A mother slipped her arm around her young colt of a son as he stepped into the aisle in front of her, and for an instant, so quick I almost missed it, he laid his head against her shoulder. An older couple held hands as they inched down the aisle. A businessman put his attache case on the seat and turned to help a college kid gather his gear. For once no one seemed to be in a hurry to make a connection or catch the first cab. The passengers walked slowly out the door. Some still wiping their eyes. Others reaching out to lift a heavy bag or help with a sleepy child.

Young . . . old . . . men . . . women . . . I watched as this small sampling of mankind left the plane. Several passengers shook my hand; others

expressed their appreciation to Father Gauthier. It was almost as if we
were leaving a church after a touching service.

I knew none of us would ever forget where we were that day in January
when Challenger exploded. In still another time of national crisis we'd
found again how much we needed, and depended upon, God. And I
knew we'd never feel closer to God than when we were part of that
prayer meeting 39,000 feet high in the Florida sky.

The combined readership of *Guideposts* and *Reader's Digest*
which are read around the world totals over 100 million people.
I had asked God to let me be a witness to thousands.

From Miami, I flew the last leg of the three-day sequence back
to Atlanta and then caught my commuter flight to the Greenville-Spartanburg Jetport. Then I climbed into my trusty Chevy
pickup and gave a sigh of relief. It was a great feeling to be going
home.

However, the Lord had other plans. Just as I was coming out
of the airport entrance road and ready to head north on I-85, He
told me, "I want you to go by the TV station, channel 16, and
share your day with the Nite Line television audience." By this
time, I was cohosting this program on almost a weekly basis.

"But, Lord," I argued, "I'm tired. I just want to go home, besides the program's already set for tonight."

But the Lord was persistent, and finally I gave up. "All right,
I'll go by the station to see how full it's booked with guests. If the
program is full, then I'll know this is not of You, and I'll go right
home." It was about an hour before "air time" when I arrived at
the station. Pam Clark, the floor director, was in the studio.

"Oh, hi, Captain Fish," she said when I walked in. "What
brings you here on your night off?"

"I don't know, Pam, maybe the Lord. How's the program
booked for tonight?" I inquired.

Her expression changed. "Terrible," she said. "One of the
guests just called in and said he can't make it, and now I have a
whole twenty minute spot open. Say," she looked over at me
again, "it couldn't be that God brought you . . ."

"I'm afraid so," I interrupted her in mid sentence. Reverend
Thompson, the host, was thrilled to have me go on with him

because his busy schedule had kept him from being fully informed of all the details of the Challenger's mishaps. As I told my story to the television audience of the call-in Christian talk show, over thirty people called and prayed with the counselors asking Jesus to become Lord of their lives. Nothing thrills my heart more than knowing that a human life has been changed through being born again by the Spirit of God. That is the greatest miracle of all. Needless to say, I didn't drive home after the program that night.

I was truly mounted on Eagle's Wings. The fingerprints of God are as soft as light—almost impossible to see or feel with the human eye, but when we look for them with our hearts, they explode into sight—full of life and love.

What's God done for you lately? More than that, what have you let Him do?